T0328455

Cambridge Elements ☰

Elements in Ancient Philosophy
edited by
James Warren
University of Cambridge

THE METHOD OF HYPOTHESIS AND THE NATURE OF SOUL IN PLATO'S *PHAEDO*

John Palmer
University of Florida

CAMBRIDGE
UNIVERSITY PRESS

CAMBRIDGE
UNIVERSITY PRESS

University Printing House, Cambridge CB2 8BS, United Kingdom

One Liberty Plaza, 20th Floor, New York, NY 10006, USA

477 Williamstown Road, Port Melbourne, VIC 3207, Australia

314–321, 3rd Floor, Plot 3, Splendor Forum, Jasola District Centre,
New Delhi – 110025, India

79 Anson Road, #06–04/06, Singapore 079906

Cambridge University Press is part of the University of Cambridge.

It furthers the University's mission by disseminating knowledge in the pursuit of
education, learning, and research at the highest international levels of excellence.

www.cambridge.org
Information on this title: www.cambridge.org/9781108930871
DOI: 10.1017/9781108946254

© John Palmer 2021

First published 2021

A catalogue record for this publication is available from the British Library.

ISBN 978-1-108-93087-1 Paperback
ISSN 2631-4118 (online)
ISSN 2631-410X (print)

The Method of Hypothesis and the Nature of Soul in Plato's *Phaedo*

Elements in Ancient Philosophy

DOI: 10.1017/9781108946254
First published online: January 2021

John Palmer
University of Florida
Author for correspondence: John Palmer, palmerj@ufl.edu

Abstract: This study of Plato's *Phaedo* promotes better understanding of its arguments for the soul's immortality by showing how Plato intended them not as proofs, but as properly dialectical arguments functioning in accordance with the method of hypothesis. Unlike the argument for the soul's immortality in the *Phaedrus*, which does seem intended as a proof, the *Phaedo* arguments are proceeding toward the first principles that could serve as the basis for a proof – the most important being an account of the soul's own essential nature. This study attends to the substantial progress the *Phaedo* makes toward such an account. It also considers Socrates' epistemic situation in the dialogue and the problem of whether his confidence in the face of death is misplaced if his arguments have not been proofs, before considering how the concluding myth draws together several of the dialogue's main themes.

Keywords: Plato, Phaedo, soul, immortality, dialectic

ISBNs: 9781108930871 (PB), 9781108946254 (OC)
ISSNs: 2631-4118 (online), 2631-410X (print)

Contents

Let it not escape us that arguments from the principles and those to the principles are different. For Plato, too, properly used to raise this problem and inquire whether we are proceeding from the ἀρχαί or to the ἀρχαί.
                                                — Aristotle, *Nicomachean Ethics* I 4.1095ᵃ30–3

1 Introduction

Not so long ago, discussions of the arguments on behalf of the soul's immortality in Plato's *Phaedo* were prone to involve the type of fallacy-hunting once a favorite sport among certain analytically inclined historians of philosophy.[1] One might reasonably wonder why in this dialogue Plato presents a string of what many have regarded as transparently poor arguments for such an important view. Presumably the reason is not because he could do no better. In the *Phaedrus* he formulates an argument on behalf of the soul's immortality generally judged superior to the arguments in the *Phaedo*. In the *Phaedrus*, Plato argues that since the nature or essence of soul is to be a self-mover, or the source and principle of its own change, it must be both ungenerated and imperishable, which is to say immortal (*Phdr.* 245c5–246a2).[2] The superiority of the *Phaedrus'* single argument to the multiple arguments of the *Phaedo* prompts a number of questions. Why do the *Phaedo*'s arguments fall short of this argument's high standard? Is there a proper philosophical explanation, as opposed to merely a developmental one? Why does the *Phaedo* present a whole series of arguments on behalf of the soul's immortality, when apparently a single argument might have sufficed? These questions may be answered, and several other issues regarding the *Phaedo*'s beleaguered arguments may be resolved, by coming to understand how the dialogue's arguments are functioning in accordance with its own method of hypothesis.

Plato is a philosopher whose writings often develop methodological and substantive concerns simultaneously and in an interconnected manner. He does so, of course, through the dramatic medium of the dialogue, whereby he engages with his readers by presenting a fictionalized discussion between a group of figures with their own characteristic perspectives and commitments. Failure to attend sufficiently to the interplay between the methodological, substantive, or dramatic dimensions of his writings is likely to result in a distorted or impoverished understanding of Plato's thought. A good deal of

---

[1] See, for example, Keyt 1963, Bostock 1986, Weller 1995.

[2] Despite its superiority, the *Phaedrus* argument has received less attention than the *Phaedo* arguments. Bett 1986 provides the best analysis along with references to earlier treatments, among which Hackforth 1952, 64–8, and Robinson 1971 may be singled out. Blyth 1997 also provides a detailed reconstruction, though the accompanying discussion is far too speculative. Mansfeld 2014 debunks the view that Plato's view of the soul as a self-mover was influenced by Alcmaeon.

attention has been paid in recent years to the significance of the dramatic and
other literary dimensions of the Platonic dialogues.[3] Although attention will be
paid here as well to the dramatic dimension of the *Phaedo*, particularly as
exemplified in the responses of its figures to the main arguments, the principal
focus will be on the interplay between the dialogue's methodological and
substantive dimensions. Attention to a Platonic dialogue's methodological
dimension is often critical for resolving apparent problems in the development
of its substantive concerns. It is especially important to bear this point in mind
when approaching the arguments of the *Phaedo*.

   One of the *Phaedo*'s outstanding problems concerns the relation between the
methodological principles articulated in Socrates' so-called intellectual autobiography (*Phd.* 95a4–102a9) and the themes pursued in the remainder of the
dialogue. While useful connections have been drawn, for instance, between
Socrates' desire for teleological explanation and the subsequent eschatological
myth,[4] and likewise between his discussion of Forms as causal or explanatory
principles and their role elsewhere in the dialogue (especially in the final
argument),[5] there is as yet insufficient appreciation of the direct connection
between the hypothetical method introduced in the autobiography and the
dialectical progression of Plato's arguments on behalf of the soul's
immortality.[6] In what follows, therefore, I articulate and explore the connection
by first drawing attention to some of the indications in the *Phaedo* that its
principal arguments are functioning as something other than proofs. I proceed to
discuss the purpose for which Plato originally introduces the hypothetical
method in the *Meno*, identify certain expectations this purpose raises with
respect to the role of this method in the *Phaedo*, and consider at some length
the extent to which these expectations are borne out by its arguments. I conclude
with some reflections on the epistemic situation of Socrates and his interlocutors
in the *Phaedo* and on the thematic role of myth in the dialogue.

   In the course of the discussion, it will become apparent that the *Phaedo*'s
arguments on behalf of the soul's immortality are "dialectical" in two senses. In
one, the primary sense, they are dialectical in that they function in accordance
with the hypothetical method of inquiry, which has by this time supplanted the
Socratic elenchus as Plato's favored mode of inquiry. They are also dialectical

---

[3] See, for example, Griswold 1988, Frede 1992, Blondell 2002. On the interplay between the
literary and philosophical aspects of the *Phaedo* in particular see Ausland 1997, Bacon 1990, and
Rowe 1993b. Rowe usefully focuses on how Socrates' interlocutors respond to his arguments.
[4] See Sedley 1991.   [5] See Politis 2010.
[6] Bedu-Addo 1979 connects Socrates' description of the hypothetical method to his description of
the philosopher's practice of death earlier in the dialogue. Kanayama 2000 tries to understand
how Socrates' descriptions of the method of hypothesis at *Phd.* 100a3–7, 101d1–e3, and 107b5–9
bear upon the final argument.

in that these arguments appear designed to provide at least some of the training in argumentation required if one is not to succumb to the distrust of reasoning or "misology" that Plato has Socrates warn against (*Phd*. 90b–e). Because the dialogue's main arguments are dialectical in these two senses, they function in subtle ways and on multiple levels that are easy to mistake or misunderstand. It should be plain that they are not meant to function as proofs of the soul's immortality, for the dialogue actually thematizes their status as something other than proofs in numerous ways. As a result, their role in supporting belief in immortality is itself problematized, though in philosophically interesting ways of which Plato himself was surely aware.

2 The Inconclusive Character of the *Phaedo*'s Arguments

Although modern commentators typically speak of the *Phaedo*'s arguments as "proofs," there are sufficient indications within the dialogue that they are not intended to function as such. One prima facie sign that they are not so designed is the presence of a series of arguments for the soul's immortality. For the purpose of proof, a single argument, such as one finds in the *Phaedrus*, would have sufficed.[7] There is evidence, moreover, that already in antiquity certain Platonists clearly appreciated that at least some of the *Phaedo*'s earlier arguments could not have been intended by Plato as decisive proofs. Thus Damascius, at the outset of his own extended treatment of the argument from opposites in his *Phaedo* commentary,[8] criticizes the explication of Iamblichus for "attempting to lend [the argument] such completeness as to constitute absolute proof of the immortality of the soul (εἰς ὅσον ἀποδεῖξαι παντελῆ τὴν ψυχῆς ἀθανασίαν), which is more than Socrates himself dared to presume it could do" (*in Phd*. I 207, trans. Westerink). Noting the way Socrates introduces the argument by asking whether they should discuss "whether these things are likely (εἰκός) to be the case or not" (*Phd*. 70b5–7), Damascius suggests instead that the argument is "true in the sense that it proves a possibility (ὡς ἀληθής τέ ἐστι καὶ ἐνδεχομένως ἀληθής)" (*in Phd*. I 207, trans. Westerink). While his characterization of the argument's positive purpose is questionable, Damascius' view that the argument is not intended to function as a decisive proof merits sympathy. One might in fact be inclined to extend something like this view to all the dialogue's arguments prior to Cebes' and Simmias' objections (*Phd*. 85e3–

---

[7] This problem motivates the proposal of Lesser 2003 that the *Phaedo* does not actually contain multiple arguments for the soul's immortality but a single argument presented in stages. Even if this proposed solution is implausible, the problem is nonetheless real.

[8] Dam. *in Phd*. I 207–52. Whereas it is now standard to see *Phd*. 70c4–72d10 as comprising three distinct arguments, Damascius speaks of them collectively as "the argument from opposites (ὁ ἀπὸ τῶν ἐναντίων λόγος)."

88b8). One might want to view them as purposely inconclusive and yet somehow preparing the reader for a final proof of the soul's immortality in the dialogue's culminating argument. Socrates' recapitulation at 95d6–e1 of Cebes' concern that fearing death is appropriate for one who does not know and cannot provide an argument that the soul is immortal (τῷ μὴ εἰδότι μηδὲ ἔχοντι λόγον διδόναι ὡς ἀθάνατόν ἐστι) might well suggest that the requisite proof is to come in the final argument.[9] Such a reading proves difficult, however, in light of the fact that Plato is careful not to present even the final argument as decisive.

The last stage of the *Phaedo*'s final argument for the soul's immortality moves from the interim conclusion regarding its not admitting the opposite of the life it brings to bodies to its being deathless and thus imperishable (105d–107a). This stage of the argument was criticized as early as the third century BC by the Peripatetic scholarch Strato of Lampsacus. He correctly drew attention to the unwarranted shift from the soul's being characterized as ἀθάνατος or "deathless," in the sense of not admitting death so long as it exists, to the claim that it is ἀνώλεθρος or unqualifiedly "imperishable." "If the negation admits multiple senses," he is reported to have objected, "the soul would be deathless, not in the sense of being inextinguishable life or possessing inextinguishable life, but in the sense that it is receptive of only one of the opposites and exists with this or does not exist."[10] Strato's point is that the most the elaborate chain of inference from *Phaedo* 102a to 105e might be thought to have shown is that a soul, so long as it exists, will no more admit death than a fire, so

---

[9] So Bedu-Addo 1979, 111, who combines this remark with Socrates' evident lack of such fear to conclude that he knows and can prove that the soul is immortal. Similarly, Sedley 2009, 146–7: "Plato created this argument and put it into Socrates' mouth precisely in order to explain why Socrates went confidently and cheerfully to his death. ... Beyond any reasonable doubt, the argument is intended to serve as *the* clinching proof of the soul's total immunity to death." See, however, the remarks at n. 13 *infra*.

[10] Strato *ap.* Dam. *in Phd.* I 433 Westerink = Strato T80 §180 Sharples. This objection appears as the third of a set of thirteen difficulties Damascius reports as having been raised by Strato against the *Phaedo*'s final argument. The eighth objection makes a similar point: "Perhaps it may have been hastily assumed that, if it is irreceptive of death and in this way deathless, it is also indestructible. For a stone also would be deathless in this way, but not indestructible" (Strato *ap.* Dam. *in Phd.* I 438 Westerink = Strato T80 §185 Sharples). See Baltussen 2015 for good discussion of the difficulties attendant upon Damascius' reports of Strato's criticisms of the *Phaedo*'s arguments. Gertz 2015 summarizes Strato's criticisms and explores Damascius' response. On the psychological theory informing Strato's criticisms, see Isnardi Parente 1977 and Modrak 2011. Sedley 1995 proposes that the summary of Socrates' arguments against Simmias' suggestion that the soul is a *harmonia* and the paraphrase of *Phaedo* 106b–e in, respectively, PHeid G inv. 28 and PGraecMon 2 (two small sets of papyrus fragments that A. Carlini in his edition at *CPF* III.7, pp. 203–20, shows to have come from a single book) may well come from the work in which Strato presented his critique of Plato's arguments for immortality in the *Phaedo*.

long as it exists, will admit cold; but this result no more entails that soul is immortal than it does that fire is inextinguishable.

This altogether appropriate objection is one Plato himself conditions his reader to make through the careful structure of question and response at the end of the argument. This dramatic dimension is regrettably lost in reconstructions that aim only to display the argument's logical structure. Socrates is quite deliberate in the culminating stage in making clear the point now at issue: whether what is deathless, in the sense in which the soul has been agreed to be deathless, is also indestructible. Thus he says to Cebes that the conclusion that the soul is not destroyed by the onset of death will follow *if* what is ἀθάνατον is also ἀνώλεθρον (106b2–3). Socrates even goes so far as to introduce a plausible objection against endorsing the conclusion based on this antecedent condition:

> But, someone might say, what prevents what is odd, while not becoming even as has been agreed, from being destroyed, and what is even coming to be instead? We could not maintain against the person who said this that it is not destroyed, for what is uneven is not indestructible. (106b7–c3)

He then restates the point at issue in even plainer terms: "So now, too, with respect to what is deathless (ἀθάνατον), *if* it is agreed by us to be also indestructible (ἀνώλεθρον), then in addition to being deathless soul would also be indestructible – but *if not*, another argument would be needed" (106c9–d1).[11]

The divergence of the interlocutors' responses at this point is crucial. Although Cebes is made to give this final step his enthusiastic endorsement, Socrates' repeated statement of the point at issue encourages readers who have carefully followed the argument to appreciate that Cebes has rashly lost sight of the sense of ἀθάνατον thus far employed: there is no need for a further argument, Cebes says, "for hardly anything else could escape destruction if *what is deathless, being everlasting* (τὸ ἀθάνατον ἀΐδιον ὄν), admits destruction" (106d2–4). Socrates, significantly, does not simply agree with Cebes' endorsement of the problematic entailment.[12] Instead, to bolster the connection he introduces a brief bit of analogical reasoning (106d5–7), which as such is hardly conclusive. Despite the assurance Socrates gives Cebes at this point, he clearly does not suppose the main argument to be unassailable.[13] His ensuing remarks to Simmias make this plain. Simmias, unlike Cebes, finds himself unprepared to

---

[11] The form of this statement echoes that which Socrates employs at 70d2–5 to introduce the cyclical arguments.

[12] Cf. Kanayama 2000, 81–2, rejecting the charge in Keyt 1963, 170–1, that Socrates commits the fallacy of equivocation.

[13] Socrates' comments at 95b8–e2 to the effect that one must be able to prove the soul immortal if one is not to be foolishly confident in the face of death are made by way of summarizing Cebes'

endorse the conclusion, even though he acknowledges not knowing just where to fault the reasoning that has led to it. Socrates responds first by commending Simmias' misgivings and then by proceeding to offer some direction on how to continue pursuing the question after he himself is gone. Plato would hardly have portrayed Socrates and Simmias responding to the final argument as he has them do if he had intended this argument to be a conclusive proof of the soul's immortality. Furthermore, Socrates' principal instructions to Simmias – that he examine the argument's initial "hypotheses" in more detail (107b5–6) – signal not only the final argument's as yet inadequate grounding but also its exemplification of the dialogue's governing method of inquiry via hypotheses.[14]

3 The Dialectical Function of the Method of Hypothesis

Plato in the *Meno* had Socrates introduce the method of hypothesis in response to Meno's desire to investigate whether ἀρετή or excellence of character is teachable. Socrates had earlier in the dialogue been unwilling to hazard any response to the question, on the grounds that he does not know what such excellence itself is and that, if he does not know what something is, then he is in no position to know what properties it possesses (*M.* 71b1–4). Toward the end of the dialogue, however, after the failure of his attempts to elicit from Meno an adequate specification of what excellence of character is, Socrates succumbed to Meno's renewed demand to address his original question of whether excellence is teachable and suggested a new way to proceed: "it seems, then, that we must inquire into *what sort of thing* something is when we do not yet know *what it is* (ποῖόν τί ἐστιν ὃ μήπω ἴσμεν ὅτι ἐστίν)" (*M.* 86d8–e1). He proposed, that is, trying to determine whether excellence of character has a certain property, namely being teachable, absent knowledge of what such excellence essentially

---

concerns about the foregoing arguments (cf. especially 88b3–6) and thus cannot be straightforwardly taken as representative of Socrates' own attitude. While Cebes' attitude as described by Socrates may well explain why Cebes is so eager to take the final argument as a decisive proof even as Socrates signals its inadequacy, Socrates' own attitude seems better represented during his earlier explanation of the philosopher's willingness to die, where he said that it is the view of the true philosophers that "so long as we have the body and our soul is suffused with an evil of this sort, we shall never possess sufficiently what we long for, and this thing we say is the truth" (66b5–7).

[14] Kanayama 2000, 86 appreciates that Socrates' recommendation to Simmias at 107b4–8 signals that the conclusion that whatever is ἀθάνατον is indestructible requires further inquiry to be properly persuasive. Dorter 2001 is also sensitive to the dynamic of the characters' response at this critical stage and takes Socrates' indication that additional argument is needed seriously enough to speculate on what it might be. The pattern of hypothetical ascent Dorter detects in the dialogue leads him to speculate that the implicit argument must be a teleological one based on a still higher hypothesis bringing in the good, such as the argument at *Timaeus* 29a–30b.

is. "So grant me one small indulgence," he said, "and allow me to conduct the inquiry by means of a hypothesis" (*M.* 86e1–3).[15]

Once they were agreed that *if excellence were a kind of knowledge*, it would be teachable (*M.* 87c5–6), Socrates and Meno proceeded to examine the hypothesis that excellence is a kind of knowledge by deploying arguments both for and against it. The argument pro the hypothesis depended on yet another hypothesis regarding the nature of excellence, namely that it is itself something good or beneficial (*M.* 87d2–3), and eventually concluded that, if excellence is beneficial, then it must be a kind of φρόνησις or wisdom (*M.* 89a1–2). The lengthy argument contra the hypothesis pointed out that there seem to be no actual teachers of excellence such as one would expect there to be if excellence were a kind of knowledge and ipso facto teachable (*M.* 89d–96c). The apparent impasse between the countervailing arguments was broken by Socrates' introduction of a point that tempered the force of the negative argument, namely that correct belief (ὀρθὴ δόξα) is as effective a guide to action as knowledge (*M.* 96d–98c). This principle makes it possible to explain how there can be excellent agents and yet no teachers of excellence while maintaining that excellence is a kind of knowledge. One should therefore expect Socrates to accept that excellence is teachable, as this accords with the stronger hypothesis. It just so happens that no one, himself included, possesses the knowledge that comprises true excellence, from which it follows that there are no actual teachers of excellence, himself included, though in principle there could be.

In the *Meno*, then, the method of hypothesis was explicitly introduced as a means of determining whether *x* has a certain property when one does not as yet know the nature or essence of *x*. The interlocutors in the *Phaedo* are in the analogous position of trying to determine whether soul has the property of immortality when they do not know the nature or essence of soul. One might then well expect the dialogue's arguments to exemplify the method of hypothesis introduced in the *Meno* as the means of approaching precisely this type of question, especially given that the central methodological portion of the *Phaedo* accords such prominence to this same method. Since the *Meno*'s application of the method of hypothesis to the question whether excellence of character is teachable leads to clarification of the nature of such excellence itself, the arguments of the *Phaedo* might be expected likewise to be leading "up"

---

[15] See Napolitano Valditara 1991 for how the *Meno* emphasizes the logical priority of the question τί ἐστιν to the question ποῖόν ἐστιν and for how it introduces inquiry via hypothesis as a heuristic method, as well as for parallels from several other dialogues. See also Benson 2015, 94–102, which acknowledges the Socratic preference for investigating the *ti* question before the *poion* question while stressing that the method of hypothesis introduced in the *Meno* to investigate the latter before the former is not presented as inferior to some preferred method.

inductively toward the kind of understanding of the soul's own nature or essence ultimately required for demonstration and knowledge of whether it is immortal. Before considering in more detail how the *Phaedo* does in fact bear out these expectations, it is worth noting that, although he explicitly introduces the method of hypothesis just prior to the final argument, Plato makes it plain enough that the method has been governing the discussion all along.

As a preface to his response to Cebes' major objection that the soul might be able to survive the demise of a series of bodies without being ultimately indestructible, Socrates describes how, when disappointed in his hope of obtaining adequate teleological explanations of natural phenomena, he embarked upon a more conceptual form of inquiry. This involved his turning away from considering entities (τὰ ὄντα σκοπῶν, 99d5) as they are directly accessible in perception to examining them indirectly in their linguistic or conceptual representations (εἰς τοὺς λόγους καταφυγόντα ἐν ἐκείνοις σκοπεῖν τῶν ὄντων τὴν ἀλήθειαν, 99e5–6). Socrates goes on to describe how this approach involved adopting as the governing hypothesis of his inquiries the assumption that there are such entities as the Beautiful itself, the Good itself, the Large itself, and so on, such that, for example, all other things that are beautiful are so in virtue of sharing in the Beautiful (100a2–c6). Although the method of hypothesis is explicitly introduced only at this important point in the dialogue (at 100a3–7), Socrates is nevertheless made to remark that this method is nothing new but something he has talked about both elsewhere *and in the discussion that has just transpired* (100b1–3).[16] He next marks the existence of intelligible Forms as his favored hypothesis: "I go back to those subjects of frequent discussion and proceed from them, hypothesizing that there is some Beautiful itself in virtue of itself (τι καλὸν αὐτὸ καθ' αὑτὸ), and a Good, a Large, and all the others"

---

[16] *Phd.* 100b1–3: "Well, he said, I mean this, nothing new, but what I've not ceased saying, both ever on other occasions and in the discussion just transpired" (Ἀλλ', ἦ δ' ὅς, ὧδε λέγω, οὐδὲν καινόν, ἀλλ' ἅπερ ἀεί τε ἄλλοτε καὶ ἐν τῷ παρεληλυθότι λόγῳ οὐδὲν πέπαυμαι λέγων). One may understand this narrowly, as indicating that his talk of Forms is nothing new (so Rowe 1993a, 241 ad loc.), or less narrowly, as an indication that what he has just described as his favored method is nothing new. Socrates has just before this acknowledged that his description of his favored method of "hypothesizing on each occasion the theory that I judge to be most powerful" (ὑποθέμενος ἑκάστοτε λόγον ὃν ἂν κρίνω ἐρρωμενέστατον εἶναι), and regarding as true or false whatever accords or fails to accord with it, requires clarification (100a3–8). The fact that the remark at 100b1–3 introduces the clarification he has just said is needed tells strongly in favor of the less narrow understanding: the description in need of clarification made no mention of Forms, and so they are unlikely to be what he has not ceased saying. Instead, the clarification itself consists principally in specifying that what he hypothesizes is that there are Forms (100b6–7). His reference to these as "those oft-mentioned entities" (ἐκεῖνα τὰ πολυθρύλητα, 100b5) may appear to favor the narrower understanding of 100b1–3, given the glancing echo of ἅπερ ... οὐδὲν πέπαυμαι λέγων. However, such a reading requires understanding 100b1–3 as looking forward to the mention of Forms in the clarification rather than back to the account of his method that he says requires clarification.

(100b4–7, cf. 76d8–9). He then says he hopes to be able, armed with this hypothesis, to cope with Cebes' lingering worries regarding the soul's immortality (100b7–9, cf. 95e8–96a1). Although Socrates in this way signals that the final argument will proceed from the hypothesized existence of Forms, his remark at 100b1–3 that the method of hypothesis is nothing new but something he has talked about in the discussion just transpired signals that it has been operative as well earlier in the dialogue.

Socrates' description of the method of hypothesis serves to clarify how the existence of intelligible Forms functions as his favored hypothesis. What it means for it to function as the governing hypothesis of his inquiries he specifies as follows: "whatever seems to me to accord with this I put down as being true, both about explanation and about everything else, and whatever does not I put down as not true" (100a5–7). Despite this rather underdetermined description, the method remains fundamentally what it was when introduced at *Meno* 86e–87a: an instrument for the inductive discovery of the first principles of demonstrative arguments.[17] From the *Meno*'s initial account of the method, taken together with its exemplification in the subsequent approach to the question whether excellence of character is teachable, one sees that to determine whether *x* is *F* when one is not yet in a position to construct a proof that would settle the issue, one first isolates a hypothesis or condition which, if satisfied, would entail that *x* is *F*. One then tries to determine whether this condition is in fact satisfied, by various means, which may include constructing arguments pro and contra the hypothesis to test whether it can be consistently maintained and/or whether it

---

[17] Late ancient philosophers, encouraged by Plato's explanation of the method of hypothesis as adapted from the geometers, would associate it with the process of analysis. On the extent to which this association is accurate, see Menn 2002. Menn argues that Plato alludes to geometrical analysis in the geometrical example of hypothetical reasoning at *M.* 86e4–87b2 and that he experimented with taking it as a model for philosophical reasoning. Karasmanis 2011 discusses the essential similarity between the method of hypothesis in the *Meno*, which Socrates indicates he is adopting from the geometers, and the method of ἀπαγωγή or "reduction" attributed to Hippocrates of Chios *ap.* Procl. *in Eucl.* 213. Aristotle himself uses the *Meno*'s argument that virtue is teachable if virtue is a kind of knowledge as an example of ἀπαγωγή and follows it with the example of Hippocrates' attempt to reduce the problem of squaring the circle (*An.Pr.* II 25.69^{b}20–37). As Menn explains, analysis involves assuming what one is trying to prove and drawing inferences from this assumption until one derives something known to be true or known to be false; the latter result constitutes a *reductio ad absurdum*, whereas the former provides the possible materials for constructing a proof if one can reverse the steps of the derivation (2002, 196–204). Although the method of hypothesis introduced in the *Meno* is not simply identical with the method of analysis, Menn is surely right to point out that the hypothesis employed in the geometrical example was "certainly found by the method of analysis, and is very typical of the use of analysis in reducing a problem to an easier problem," and he thus concludes that "since Plato is recommending a method for finding appropriate hypotheses and so reducing hard questions to easier ones, it is analysis that he is recommending" (2002, 212). See also the more recent treatments of the method of hypothesis in the *Meno* and the geometrical example used to introduce it in Iwata 2015.

might be better formulated, and then by trying to isolate some prior or more fundamental condition(s) that, if satisfied, would entail this hypothesis. Of course, in identifying the prior condition(s), one is attempting to arrive at something that has already been securely established. The analytic function and "upward-leading" character of the method of hypothesis are even more prominent in the way it features at *Republic* 510b–511e in the simile of the divided line. In the *Phaedo*, this function and character come to the fore when Socrates completes his description of the method:

> If someone were to seize upon the hypothesis itself, you would let him alone and not respond until you examined whether the things that proceed from it accord with each other or are in disaccord.[18] Then when you need to give an account of that hypothesis itself, you would do so in the same way, hypothe-sizing yet another hypothesis that seems the best of those above, until you come to something sufficient. (101d3–8)

This description, reminiscent of the method's exemplification in the *Meno*, indicates how to reach a point where one's justification is no longer based merely on hypotheses but is securely established and can be displayed in the form of a demonstration or proof.[19]

---

[18] The words ἕως ἂν τὰ ἀπ᾽ ἐκείνης ὁρμηθέντα σκέψαιο εἴ σοι ἀλλήλοις συμφωνεῖ ἢ διαφωνεῖ have occasioned a good deal of discussion and disagreement. Understanding τὰ ἀπ᾽ ἐκείνης ὁρμηθέντα as the hypothesis' logical consequences or entailments and συμφωνεῖ and διαφωνεῖ as respectively marking logical consistency and inconsistency seems not to make for a sensible methodological recommendation and is hard to square with Socrates' initial description of the hypothetical method at 100a3–7. Commentators have consequently sought alternative construals of these key terms. See Gentzler 1991 for the proposal that συμφωνεῖν in the two passages marks a relation stronger than mere logical consistency yet weaker than entailment. See Ebert 2001 and Fischer 2002 for further discussion. Bailey 2005 takes Gentzler's proposal as the principal point of departure for an interpretation stressing συμφωνεῖν's musical overtones to suggest that the relevant relation is one of providing the sort of mutual explanatory support that relates general and more particular claims. One lesson to be taken from the discussion is that Plato's terminology is less technical and logically precise than one might have wished. Translating συμφωνεῖ and διαφωνεῖ as "accord" and "are in disaccord," as here, in the first place gives συμφωνεῖν a sense that also works well for its usage at 100a5, where Socrates says he counts as true whatever he thinks συμφωνεῖν or "accords" with his favored hypothesis, for one may take an account or explanation to accord with a hypothesis when generally governed by it. The intervening discussion of the kinds of explanatory accounts Socrates has come to prefer in accordance with the hypothesis that entities other than the Form of *F*-ness are *F* because they participate in the Form of *F*-ness (100c3–101d2) exemplifies what he means by an account according with a hypothesis (cf. Bedu-Addo 1979, 116–18). As for what is meant by examining whether the consequences of a hypothesis are in accord or in disaccord, it is best to look to the *Meno*'s examination of the hypothesis that virtue is a kind of knowledge, where the construction of arguments pro and contra the hypothesis gives the appearance of discordant results that must be resolved for the hypothesis to survive.

[19] Based on the descriptions of the method of hypothesis in the *Meno* and *Phaedo*, Benson 2015, 114–15, identifies it as involving a "proof stage" and a "confirmation stage" and discusses the details of its procedures in the remainder of ch. 5. In approaching a question

One obvious difference between the method of hypothesis as exemplified in the *Meno* and *Phaedo* is that in the *Meno* the method of hypothesis more clearly involves the reduction of one question to another as a technique for the development of a proof. The original question as to whether virtue is teachable is reduced, via the hypothesis that virtue is teachable if (and only if) it is a kind of knowledge, to the question as to whether virtue is a kind of knowledge. These questions are not simply equivalent; for not only do they mean different things but the point that virtue is a kind of knowledge is also introduced as a possible basis for the point that virtue is teachable. Furthermore, the point that virtue is a kind of knowledge itself contains the beginning of a specification of the nature of virtue itself.[20] In the *Phaedo*, however, the method of hypothesis as described by Socrates does not obviously involve the reduction of one question to another in this way, nor does the Forms hypothesis Socrates indicates he favors point toward what the soul might be as obviously as the *Meno*'s hypothesis pointed to what virtue itself might be. I nevertheless want to claim that the method of hypothesis as employed in the *Phaedo* remains what it was in the *Meno*, a method for the discovery of proof by proceeding toward first principles. Here the requisite first principle is a specification of the nature of soul, insofar as one needs to know first what the soul is in order to know whether it is immortal, even as in the *Meno* Socrates appreciates that one must know what virtue is in order to know whether it is teachable.

When Socrates says, then, at *Phaedo* 100b1–3 that the method of hypothesis is nothing new but something that he has both discussed before and that has been governing the discussion to this point, his remark signals that the discussion has been proceeding analytically and inductively to the isolation of ever

---

such as whether virtue is teachable or whether the soul is immortal, the proof stage involves identifying a second question, the most compelling answer to which is to serve as a hypothesis from which an answer to that original question may be obtained and showing how so. The confirmation stage involves testing the hypothesis and proceeding to a higher hypothesis if necessary until one reaches something adequate, in the way described at *Phaedo* 101d3–8. Whereas the *Meno* partially exemplifies both stages Benson identifies, the *Phaedo* does not exemplify what he calls the confirmation stage since the existence of Forms remains a hypothesis throughout the dialogue and is not itself tested or grounded upon any higher principle. That testing and grounding appears to occur in the *Parmenides*, where the discussion can be seen as conforming to Socrates' description here in the *Phaedo* of how to proceed if someone challenges one's hypothesis. Benson 2015, ch. 7, takes the hypothetical method to be exemplified in the *Phaedo* only in the discussion of Forms as *aitia* at 100a8–101d1, and not even in the fuller argument to which that discussion belongs. This view seems unduly restrictive, however, and it will hopefully become clear that there is good reason to take all of the arguments in the dialogue governed by the Forms hypothesis as operating in accordance with the method described at *Phd.* 100a–b and d, and that there are even grounds for seeing it as operative in the discussion of the prohibition of suicide.

[20] On these points, contrast the views advanced in Ebrey 2013.

more fundamental bases for determining the truth of the questions being addressed. It is apparent in retrospect that the dialogue's discussion of philosophical issues bearing upon death and the fate of the soul – beginning straight off with the initial treatment of the prohibition against suicide – has in fact followed an upward dialectical progression in accordance with the basic principles of the method of hypothesis.

4 Dialectical Progression in the Discussion of Suicide

The discussion of the prohibition against suicide[21] involves the initial isolation of a hypothesis that, if satisfied, would entail that suicide is unlawful, followed by a problematization of the hypothesis that draws attention to its apparent inconsistency with the discussants' other commitments. An effort is then made to resolve this appearance of inconsistency by focusing on a new demonstrandum, first via a hypothesis regarding the nature of death, then via what proves to be Socrates' favored hypothesis. This new hypothesis regarding the nature of death is in turn problematized in a way that yields the principal demonstranda for the arguments to come, namely that the soul is not destroyed at death and that it continues to possess its capacity for understanding after being separated from the body. Socrates and Cebes' discussion of the prohibition against suicide thus prepares us for the major series of arguments to follow regarding the soul's immortality. The discussion proceeds generally in the upward direction characteristic of hypothetical inquiry, thereby isolating ever more fundamental questions regarding the soul and eventually introducing Socrates' preferred hypothesis. The structure of the progression is made clear when displayed as follows:

DEMONSTRANDUM:	It is not lawful for a person to kill himself (61e5–6).
HYPOTHESIS:	Humans are in the charge of the gods (62b7–8).
ARGUMENT:	The gods would not permit their charges to kill themselves without permission (62c1–8).

---

[21] The subtleties of this discussion are thoughtfully explored by Warren 2001 with a view to understanding why a Platonist accepting the main tenets of the *Phaedo* associated with the preferability of the discarnate soul over the incarnate soul should not always prefer being dead to being alive. Warren emphasizes how the discussion points to the need to attend to the character of a person's life in order to draw the relevant and necessary distinction between the philosopher's willingness to die (embodied in the person of Socrates) and the suicides prohibited to others, and he suggests that the *Phaedo* does ultimately suggest the requisite distinction between "the unphilosophical short cut to the separation of body and soul and the gradual philosophical purification of the soul and removal of bodily concerns which occurs throughout a life" (102), such that it is only rational to opt for death when one's soul has been purified as far as possible in life from its association with the body.

Objection by Cebes: Socrates' claim that the philosopher is ready and willing to die conflicts with this hypothesis (62c9–e7, cf. 61d3–5).

DEMONSTRANDUM:	The philosopher should welcome death (62c10–d1).
HYPOTHESIS:	Death is the soul's separation from the body (64c4–5).
ARGUMENT A:	The philosopher does not concern himself with what belongs to the body but instead strives throughout his life to purify his soul from its association with the body while alive (64c10–65a8). Implied conclusion: The philosopher should welcome death as being the total separation of the soul from the body.
ARGUMENT B:	The philosopher's desire to achieve understanding, to grasp the truth, and to apprehend reality is most fully achieved while alive when he is able to free his soul from its association with the body so that it can operate "itself by itself" (65a9–c10). Therefore, the philosopher's soul, disregarding the body and fleeing from it, seeks to become "itself by itself" (65c11–d2); that is, it longs for the complete separation from the body involved in being dead.

An additional *hypothesis* is now introduced for the third in this series of arguments, namely:

HYPOTHESIS:	There is a Justice itself, and a Beautiful, a Good, and all the rest (65d4–e1, cf. 100b4–7).
ARGUMENT C:	"Whoever of us prepares himself best and most accurately to grasp that thing itself which he is investigating [i.e. the relevant Form] will come closest to the knowledge of it. .... Then he will be able to do this most perfectly who approaches the object with thought alone, without associating any sight with his thought, or dragging in any sense perception with his reasoning, but who, using *pure thought alone*, tries to track down *each reality pure and by itself*, freeing himself as far as possible from eyes and ears, and in a word, from the whole body, because the body confuses the soul and does not allow it to acquire truth and wisdom whenever it is associated with it" (65e2–66a5, trans. Grube). The implicit conclusion is that the philosopher's longing for truth and understanding is in effect a longing for the complete separation of the soul from the body, which is death.

Objection by Cebes (69d6–70b4): When the soul is separated from the body it may no longer exist anywhere but be destroyed and perish when the person dies (70a2–6).

MAJOR DEMONSTRANDUM:	The soul is not destroyed at death.
MINOR DEMONSTRANDUM:	The soul continues to possess its capacity for intelligence after separation from the body at death (70b2–4).

Socrates and Cebes begin by considering the thesis that it is not lawful for a person to kill himself (61e5–6). The prohibition against suicide enters the discussion as a Pythagorean teaching.[22] Socrates stresses that his own knowledge of this subject is based on what he has heard from others (61d9–10). Socrates' contribution will be, as he says, to show that what may seem surprising or even unreasonable perhaps does have a certain rationale (ἴσως γ' ἔχει τινὰ λόγον, 62b1–2). He approaches this task by identifying a condition that, if satisfied, would mean that the prohibition against suicide is itself justified. From certain "sacred writings" or Orphic texts, which teach that the body is for human beings a sort of prison[23] from which they are not to escape on their own, Socrates adopts the notion that *humans are the charges of and belong to the gods*, something Cebes accepts (*Phd.* 62b2–10). The prohibition against suicide thus becomes readily comprehensible, since the gods would presumably not want their charges to do away with themselves (62c1–8). At the end of this simple argument, Cebes comments that this conclusion appears likely or reasonable (εἰκός, 62c9), even though an objection immediately occurs to him. The argumentation here begins the pattern of ascent that will be employed throughout the remainder of the central discussion. First, a demonstrandum is introduced. Then a further thesis is introduced as a plausible basis on which to construct an argument supporting it. The grounding claim, however, is clearly only a hypothesis – for while, if true, it would entail the demonstrandum, its own

---

[22] Socrates says that Cebes and Simmias might have heard it from the Pythagorean Philolaus (61d6–7, cf. e7). Cebes acknowledges he did hear Philolaus speak of this during his visit to Thebes, though Cebes also says that he has not heard from Philolaus or anyone else a clear explanation of the prohibition (61e6–8).

[23] The term φρουρά can have the sense of "watch" or "guard-duty" as well as that of "prison," but the context makes the latter sense far more likely here, as does the familiarity from Plato of the Orphic view that embodiment is for the soul a kind of imprisonment (cf. Pl. *G.* 493a1–3, *Crat.* 400c1–10). See Rowe 1993a, 128 *ad* 62b3–5, Edmonds 2004, 176–8, and 2013, 269–72. For a review of earlier discussion on the issue and a defense of understanding φρουρά as "prison," see Strachan 1970. Warren 2001, 97 n. 15, notes that "the clear and immediate link between Socrates' current position, and the idea of incarnation as imprisonment" tells in favor of this understanding and likewise cites several allusions to this stretch of the *Phaedo* in Cicero and Augustine reflecting the notion of imprisonment.

status is as yet insecure. In this instance, its derivation from the Orphic teaching that the soul's embodiment is a kind of imprisonment, the way it is secured for the purpose of the argument merely by Socrates' and Cebes' agreement, and the way Socrates marks the conclusion of the argument based upon it as "perhaps not without reason" (ἴσως ... οὐκ ἄλογον, 62c6) all serve to indicate that the grounding claim is at best an apparently plausible hypothesis.

The hypothesis itself, moreover, is immediately subjected to examination after the argument's conclusion, and in just the way Socrates subsequently indicates one must consider hypotheses themselves, namely by examining whether their consequences are in accord (101d4–6). Cebes objects that if indeed it is reasonable (εἴπερ ... εὐλόγως ἔχει) that God is our overseer and we his possessions, then it is not reasonable (οὐκ ἔχει λόγον) for an intelligent person not to be distressed about having to leave the service of the best possible masters; and Cebes concludes that this result contradicts Socrates' previous claim that those who are genuine philosophers should be ready and willing to die (62c9–e7). This objection hearkens back to the tension Cebes had originally detected between the advice Socrates bid him pass along to Evenus – to follow him soon once he himself has departed this life – and his remark that taking one's own life is supposed to be illicit (61b7–d5). If God is our master, then unbidden suicide will be impermissible, *and* we should want to continue our service to our divine master as long as possible. The latter entailment conflicts with the otherwise independent claim that a genuine philosopher will die readily and willingly.

The way Cebes seizes upon the hypothesis and calls attention to its apparent conflict with earlier claims notably elicits Socrates' approval. In a momentary recursion of the dialogue frame, Phaedo remarks that he thought Socrates seemed pleased with Cebes' πραγματεία or attentive treatment of the topic (62e8–63a1). Socrates is himself made to remark that Cebes is always keen on examining arguments and will at first be disinclined to believe whatever one says (63a1–3). In addition to establishing what is perhaps the keynote in the dialogue's characterization of Cebes, Socrates' remark highlights the complex relation between argument and belief that will become an ever more significant theme as the dialogue progresses. Here Cebes displays some of the dialectical sophistication or skill required to avoid the experience that will later be described as engendering distrust of all argument. His ability to identify how the hypothesized principle that humans belong to the gods entails something that contradicts another of his interlocutor's claims – just the kind of dialectical skill characteristic of Socrates himself in the so-called elenctic dialogues – prevents Cebes from succumbing to belief in an as yet inadequately established thesis. This initial representation of Cebes may make his eventual reaction to the final argument appear all the more surprising. For there he wholeheartedly endorses a conclusion Socrates is rather careful to mark as inadequately secured by the argument just given. This tension between Cebes' reactions to the dialogue's first and last arguments is just one of the numerous ways the dialogue highlights the complex relation between argument and belief, though this is not the point to delve into that complex aspect of the dialogue. At the moment, we need to continue tracking the discussion's ascent toward more fundamental questions and higher hypotheses.

Cebes' objection has the effect of making a new demonstrandum of Socrates' previous claim that a philosopher should welcome death. As Socrates picks up the discussion with Simmias, the two agree that death is the soul's separation from the body, such that being dead involves the body having come to exist apart and having come to be itself by itself separate from the soul, with the soul likewise existing apart and being itself by itself separate from the body (64c2–9).[24] These specifications provide the foundations for Socrates' ensuing series of three arguments that philosophy is a kind of preparation for death, in that the philosopher, even in life, seeks to purify and separate the soul as much as possible from its association with the body and bodily concerns. The first two of these arguments proceed directly from the hypothesis that death is the soul's separation from the body. Socrates argues, first, that the philosopher does not concern himself with what belongs to the body but instead strives throughout his life to purify his soul from its association with the body (64c10–65a8). The implicit conclusion is that the philosopher should welcome death as the total separation of the soul from the body. Next, Socrates argues that the philosopher's desire to achieve understanding, grasp the truth, and apprehend reality is most fully achieved while alive when he is able to free his soul from its association with the body so that it can operate αὐτὴ καθ' αὑτήν or "on its own" (65a9–c10), which is to say independently of the body, in the pure activity of thought and understanding, rather than in association with the body, as in perception. The philosopher's soul, consequently, disregards and flees from the body while seeking to exist "on its own" (αὐτὴ καθ' αὑτήν, 65c11–d2), and

---

[24] It is sometimes thought that this specification of what death is prejudges the question of its survival after death. See the second difficulty raised at Gallop 1975, 86–7 ad loc. But the account of death as the soul's separation from the body functions here merely as a hypothesis, secured merely by Simmias' and Socrates' agreement; it will rightly be called into question by Cebes at 70a2–6, as is properly noted by Rowe 1993a, 136–7, *ad* 64c4–5, though Rowe finds the soul's survival illicitly presumed in what follows (compare Gallop's fifth difficulty at p. 87). Sedley 1995, 15, points out that Socrates deliberately addresses his question here to Simmias rather than Cebes because Simmias can be relied upon to agree, and it suits Socrates' strategy to delay the question of whether the soul is such as to survive death.

this attitude is implicitly understood as tantamount to longing for the soul's complete separation from the body in death.

The third and final argument of this series is noteworthy for its introduction of an additional hypothesis – precisely the one Socrates subsequently singles out as his preferred hypothesis – namely, that there are Forms of Justice, Beauty, Goodness, and the rest. He begins here by asking Simmias: "Do we say there is some Just itself or not?" (65d4–5). When Simmias replies that "we" do indeed say this, Socrates asks: "And some Beautiful as well and a Good?" (65d7). Simmias again agrees. Socrates then begins to ask how one best apprehends these entities and expands the list by saying, "I'm speaking about all these things, including Greatness, Health, Strength, and, in a word, about the essence of all the other things that each thing happens to be (τῆς οὐσίας ὃ τυγχάνει ἕκαστον ὄν)" (65d12–e1). This first introduction of Forms into the discussion will be alluded to later in the autobiography when Socrates describes his favorite hypothesis: "I go back to those things we always keep talking about and start from them, hypothesizing that there is some Beautiful itself in itself and a Good, a Great, and all the rest" (100b4–7). That the existence of Forms functions here in the third argument for the claim that a philosopher should welcome death purely as an as yet ungrounded hypothesis is already clear enough from the abrupt manner in which the existence of Forms is introduced, with no explanation or justification, simply as a point on which Socrates and Simmias are agreed.[25]

Armed with this powerful hypothesis, Socrates proceeds to argue that that person will be best prepared to apprehend the nature of each of these Forms who approaches them with the intellect on its own, divorced as far as possible from the hampering effects of bodily sensation (65e1–66a8). The implicit conclusion is once again that the philosopher should welcome death. The way Socrates is made to put his point suggests some variety of assimilation of the intellect to its objects, the Forms, in respect of their purity and isolation from bodily association: "employing the intellect itself on its own and uncorrupted, he would

---

[25] The use of φαμέν in Socrates' initial question, "Do we say (φαμέν) there is some Just itself or not?" (65d4–5), as well as in Simmias' emphatic response, "Of course we say so, by Zeus" (Φαμέν μέντοι νὴ Δία, 65d6), may accordingly appear to border on having the more technical sense of "posit." It is similarly used to introduce the unargued assumption at the outset of the recollection argument that there is an Equal itself, with Simmias still more emphatically acknowledging in response to Socrates that "we say" (Φῶμεν) there is such a thing (74b1). Elsewhere, Plato has Socrates employ "we say" (φαμέν) when referring to a presumed general agreement to secure his point. So, for example, at *Euthyphr.* 13a4: "for example, we say (φαμέν) that not everyone knows how to care for horses, but the horseman does, don't we?" The fact that the "we" is more narrowly, though somewhat indeterminately, circumscribed – including at least Socrates and Simmias, but apparently others with similar sympathies, though certainly not people generally – is what gives these usages their apparently more technical sense.

endeavor to detect each of these realities itself on its own and uncorrupted (αὐτῇ καθ' αὑτὴν εἰλικρινεῖ τῇ διανοίᾳ χρώμενος αὐτὸ καθ' αὑτὸ εἰλικρινὲς ἕκαστον ἐπιχειροῖ θηρεύειν τῶν ὄντων)" (66a1–3). This likening of the soul in its cognitive dimension to the Forms as the proper objects of its cognition involves an implicit assimilation of the soul or mind to its objects that anticipates features of the subsequent affinity argument for the soul's immortality. In doing so, this third argument in support of the claim that the philosopher should welcome death is starting to move in the direction of clarifying the nature of the soul itself, something that becomes an ever more fundamental concern as the dialectical ascent continues through the arguments on behalf of the soul's immortality.

Soon after the discussion of the prohibition against suicide, at the point of transition from Socrates' defense of the philosophical life to the series of arguments for the soul's immortality, Cebes once again spurs articulation of a new demonstrandum, this time via an objection to the recently operative hypothesis. He expresses his concern about the way Socrates and Simmias had earlier defined death and being dead (at 64c2–9), saying that when the soul is separated from the body it may no longer exist anywhere but be destroyed and perish when the person dies (69e7–70b4). Although some characterize Cebes as simply objecting that the definition of death as the soul's separation of the body is question-begging, doing so fails to appreciate fully the dialectical function of Cebes' objection. Socrates and Simmias have in effect accepted the definition of death as the soul's separation from the body as a hypothesis. Socrates then proceeds to argue that, if this is what death is, then it is right to see philosophy as preparation for death and right for the philosopher to be sanguine about his prospects after death. Cebes' objection then prompts examination of the hypothesis itself. He is even made to mark the still conditional status of the conclusions Socrates has drawn: "For *if indeed* [the soul] were somewhere gathered together on its own and released from these evils which you just now described, there would be a great and noble hope, Socrates, that what you're saying is true" (70a6–b1). And he calls explicitly for an examination of the as yet merely hypothesized antecedent of this conditional: "But indeed this perhaps requires no small amount of reassurance (παραμυθία) and convincing (πίστις), that the soul both exists once the person is dead and possesses some capacity and intelligence" (70b1–4). From Cebes' objection there once again comes a new demonstrandum (more accurately, a pair of demonstranda) that becomes the focus of the subsequent argument. Socrates' question to Cebes at this point of transition, "Do you wish us to engage in a discussion (διαμυθολογῶμεν) about precisely these matters, to see whether they are likely (εἰκός) to be the case or not?" (70b6–7), is yet another indication that Plato does not intend the ensuing arguments to function as proofs. Instead, as will be seen, these arguments continue the dialectical progression toward ever more fundamental matters in accordance with the method of hypothesis.

5 The Dialectical Function of the Cyclical Arguments

Among the series of arguments that now follow in quick succession, only the cyclical arguments do not rely upon the existence of Forms as their hypothesis. They are also concerned only with the first of the pair of demonstranda isolated by Cebes' most recent objection, namely that the soul continues to exist once the person is dead. Socrates and Cebes approach the claim that the soul is not destroyed at death (70c4–5) by isolating as an antecedent demonstrandum the claim that the living are born from nowhere else than the dead (70c5–d2). In much the same way as the prohibition against suicide earlier entered the discussion as a Pythagorean teaching, this claim is introduced on the basis of an "ancient story" that told of how souls travel from here to Hades and return here reborn from the dead. The isolation of this antecedent demonstrandum conforms more or less directly to the analytical approach integral to the method of hypothesis, wherein one proceeds by identifying and then examining a proposition from which one's principal demonstrandum would follow. If it could actually be made evident, Socrates says, that the living are born from the dead, it would furnish a sufficient indication[26] that the soul exists in Hades; if not, he says, another argument would be needed (70d2–5). Plato here has Socrates express reservation about whether he and Cebes will in fact be able to establish securely that the living are born from the souls of the dead, and the cyclical arguments in fact prove to be something of a false start. Their principal function in the dialogue's dialectical progression is to provide certain positive, if cautionary, lessons regarding both the selection of a hypothesis in approaching the main question and what one's focus needs to be in seeking to resolve it.

The governing hypothesis of the first cyclical argument (70c8–71e3) is inductively established on the basis of a series of examples. The hypothesis that emerges is a perfectly general principle regarding change, according to which "opposites come from opposites" (70e1–2). More precisely, for any pair of opposite attributes, F and opp-F, x comes to be F only from being opp-F and opp-F only from being F (70e4–6; cf. 71a9–10). A corollary to this principle is

---

[26] Gallop 1975, 16, translates ἱκανὸν τεκμήριον as "sufficient evidence," which is, like "a sufficient indication" here, preferable to Grube's over-translation "sufficient proof." The other occurrences of τεκμήριον in the *Phaedo* are at 87b7 and, modified by ἱκανόν as here, at 68b8, 72a6, and 96c3–4. In the last of these passages, τεκμήριον clearly has the sense of "evidence" rather than proof or argument. The sense of τεκμήριον in the *Phaedo* is fixed by that of the cognate verb τεκμαίρομαι, as the sign or evidence on which one bases one's judgment.

also introduced, according to which there are always two contrary changes between F and opp-F: from F to opp-F and from opp-F to F (71a12–b2). Since this corollary furnishes the main premise of the second cyclical argument (71e4–72a10), and its denial serves as the basis for a *reductio* in the third argument, the general principle may be regarded as governing all three arguments in this series. From the general principle regarding change between opposites and the additional premise that being dead is the opposite of being alive, the first argument concludes that living things come to be from the dead. From the corollary to the general principle and the additional premise that we observe the generation of the dead from the living, the second argument concludes that there must likewise be generation of the living from the dead and thus that the souls of the dead must exist somewhere. The third argument (72a11–e2), finally, assuming the denial of the corollary, argues that if the change between being alive and being dead proceeded only in this one direction, then eventually all things would end up being dead. Although the conclusion is not explicitly drawn, this result is apparently regarded as somehow impossible, so that there must be a corresponding change between being dead and being alive.

While the examples of opposites given at the point of the general principle's initial formulation (70e2–3) are beautiful and ugly and just and unjust, the qualities adduced to provide the inductive support for its more precise formulation are notably all comparatives: larger and smaller, stronger and weaker, slower and faster, and so on (70e6–71a8). Although it is tautological that something can only become more F from a prior condition of being less F than it comes to be, the initial formulation of the governing hypothesis is subject to obvious counterexamples, most conspicuously in Socrates' own initial examples. For someone or something may become beautiful or just without having previously been positively the opposite of beautiful, that is, ugly, or the opposite of just, that is, unjust. One might counter that to become beautiful or just requires previously being not-beautiful or not-just. However, the argument concerns opposites, and not-beautiful and not-just are not the opposites of beautiful and just.[27] It is therefore clear that Cebes assents too readily when Socrates asks whether the general principle regarding change on which the first two cyclical arguments are based has been sufficiently (ἱκανῶς)

---

[27] Sedley 2012, 150–5, commenting on *Phd.* 70d7–71b4, properly notes that while the opposites are named in their noncomparative forms, Plato uses comparatives when describing the changes between them. This point leads to effective criticisms of the common view that the opposites here are contradictories. Sedley ultimately identifies the opposites here with what he calls "converse contraries," such that F and G are contraries and x is F compared with y iff y is G compared with x.

established by this survey of examples (71a9–11).[28] There are obvious counter-examples as well to the corollary to the general principle: between the opposites young and old, for instance, there is only one direction of change.[29] Cebes appears not to consider whether there might be opposites that do not conform to the general principle, even though the very qualities Socrates uses to explain what he means by "opposites" – beautiful and ugly and just and unjust – fail so to conform. The lesson might seem to be that a hypothesis should itself receive due consideration – by considering, for instance, what can be said against as well as for it – before arguments are built upon it. Later in the dialogue, Socrates may be indirectly commenting on the inadequacy of the cyclical arguments' general principle regarding change when he tells Cebes that a general account of coming to be and perishing is required to deal adequately with his objection that the soul might undergo numerous reincarnations and yet still be eventually destroyed (95e9–96a1). The attentive reader has in any case already been prompted by Plato to recognize the inadequacy of the cyclical arguments' governing hypothesis by the examples of opposites given by Socrates as he formulates the principle. It is thus no surprise that the subsequent arguments deploy a new hypothesis.

Even more importantly, certain of the cyclical arguments' inadequacies highlight the need for the interlocutors to get clearer about the nature of soul itself in considering whether or not it is immortal. In the first argument, even if Cebes too readily accepts the analysis of change between opposites as a general principle, it could still apply in the particular case of the opposites

---

[28] Although he notes that Plato here employs noncomparative and comparative terms for opposites, Sedley 2012, 156–8, supposes they are effectively synonymous, "there being no essential difference between 'x is larger than y' and 'x is large compared with y'," and he proceeds to develop on Plato's behalf a "comparative analysis of change," such that, for example, in growth a subject goes from being smaller to larger. However, since alive and dead are opposites that do not admit of degrees and thus do not have comparative forms, the comparative analysis of change will not apply in their case and thus seems unlikely to be the analysis Plato has in mind. While Sedley recognizes this obvious problem for his account, his attempts to deal with it are not altogether successful. An alternative (suggested to me by James Warren) would be to suppose that *Phd.* 66a–67b introduced a conception of being dead such that it does admit of degrees, insofar as the philosopher's purified soul is more separate from the body of the non-philosopher's soul. This suggestion plays on Plato's own characterization of death as the separation of the soul from the body (64c4–5), though Plato goes on to specify this as the soul's *total* separation from the body and vice versa (c5–8), and this in fact seems to be the relevant sense of dead in the arguments at this point in the dialogue. The problem in any case remains that it is in fact exceedingly difficult to specify what Plato means by opposites here in a way that will apply to all his examples, while also providing a formulation of the argument's general principle that will properly apply to opposites so specified and particularly to the opposites alive and dead. See the attempt by Barnes 1978 (reviewing Gallop 1975) and the critical response in Gallop 1982.

[29] This obvious objection features as the fifth of the seven difficulties Damascius lists as having been raised by Strato against the argument from opposites: "If people become old from young, but not vice versa" (Strato *ap*. Dam. *in Phd.* II 63 Westerink = Strato T76 §5 Sharples).

living and being dead. It does so happen to apply in the case of the opposites waking and sleeping, which Socrates introduces to spur Cebes' response that being dead is the opposite of living (71c1–5). A person can only come to be awake from a prior condition of being asleep (and vice versa). The principle interestingly applies in this case even though waking and sleeping are not comparative qualities of the sort that make the principle tautological. At this stage of the argument, however, it is more important to note how treating living and being dead as analogous to waking and sleeping highlights the very real problems in identifying the *subject of the change* from being alive to being dead. For this change is decidedly unlike the change from waking to sleeping (and vice versa), where the subject is readily identified as some person or animal. It is surely no accident that Plato has Socrates solicit Cebes' agreement in this argument's final steps at 71d5–e3 in an otherwise inexplicably laborious fashion that studiously avoids any mention of *what* is supposed to come to be alive from being dead (and vice versa):

So then *you* tell me, Socrates said, just the same about life and death. Do you not say that being dead (τὸ τεθνάναι) is the opposite of being alive (τῷ ζῆν)?
I do.

And that they come to be from one another?
Yes.

What is it, then, that comes to be from what is alive (ἐξ ... τοῦ ζῶντος)?
What is dead (τὸ τεθνηκός), Cebes said.

And what is it, Socrates said, that comes to be from what is dead (ἐκ τοῦ τεθνεῶτος)?
It is necessary to agree, he said, that it is what is alive (τὸ ζῶν).

Is it the case, Cebes, that living things and living subjects (τὰ ζῶντά τε καὶ οἱ ζῶντες) come to be from the dead?
It appears to be (φαίνεται), Cebes said.

Is it then the case, Socrates said, that our souls exist in Hades?
It seems so (ἔοικεν).

The penultimate conclusion here is, of course, the antecedent demonstrandum initially identified by Socrates and Cebes at 70c5–d2, while the final conclusion is the main demonstrandum that the soul continues to exist once the individual person is dead. Unlike in the case where the sleeping come to be from the waking (and vice versa), one cannot say that the dead individual comes to be from the living individual (and vice versa), unless, perhaps, the individual is somehow identified with the soul. But to speak of the soul itself as the subject that changes from living to being dead conflicts prima facie with the main demonstrandum that the soul is not destroyed at death. A "dead soul" would seem to be a soul no longer.

There is a similar problem in the third cyclical argument. Without the assumption of a substrate soul alternately coming to be alive and being dead, this argument only proves that there is some process whereby things come to be alive, though not necessarily from the reincarnation of souls. Nothing here rules out some type of emergence, where life is not brought to the appropriate organic material by any preexisting entity but simply arises in such material when properly constituted. Thus the argument cannot stand as a proof of immortality, for it seems to beg the question. Like the other cyclical arguments, it nonetheless has an identifiable function within the dialogue's dialectical progression, namely to impress on Plato's readers the need to get clearer about just what it is that potentially persists through the change a person undergoes at death. A genuine demonstration of whether or not the soul is immortal requires a clearer understanding of the nature of the entity whose continued existence after death is at issue.[30]

Plato must have been aware of the problems with the cyclical arguments to which we have here drawn attention because the subsequent arguments rely on a different hypothesis, the existence of Forms, and eventually focus on clarifying the nature of the soul itself. He also structures his characters' responses so as to encourage his readers to attend to the cyclical arguments' inadequacies and thereby to think more deeply about what an adequate demonstration of the soul's immortality would require. Thus, for instance, despite his apparently rash endorsement of the general principle regarding change on which these arguments are based, the reader finds Cebes responding more tentatively, even grudgingly, as the first cyclical argument proceeds, until in the end he gives its conclusions only the weakest of endorsements.[31] Cebes' reservation at the end of the second argument is even more pronounced. He says only that he thinks the conclusions necessarily follow from what has been agreed (δοκεῖ μοι ... ἐκ τῶν ὡμολογημένων ἀναγκαῖον οὕτως ἔχειν, 72a9–10). Socrates' remarks spur concerns of a different sort. At the end of the second argument he echoes his prefatory comment at 70d2–5 by noting that he and Cebes are here again agreed that the living have been born from the dead and that they had

---

[30] Pakaluk 2003 argues that if one assumes a substance dualism, according to which every living thing has a soul that is a distinct substance from the body, such that being dead and being alive can be specified as properties of soul, then many of the standard objections to the cyclical arguments fail. Although Pakaluk finds an affirmation of substance dualism in Socrates' earlier defense of the philosophical life, it certainly does not feature in the cyclical arguments themselves, which studiously avoid any sort of specification of what the soul is.

[31] Cf. Rowe 1993a, 159 *ad* 71d13, and 1993b, 171–3.

thought that, if this should be the case, it would be a sufficient indication (ἱκανόν . . . τεκμήριον) that of necessity the souls of the dead exist somewhere, from whence they are once again born (72a4–8). He decidedly does not say that the second cyclical argument is a sufficient proof of the soul's immortality. He merely reiterates that the principal demonstrandum that the soul is not destroyed at death follows from the antecedent demonstrandum that the living are born from the dead, and he notes that Cebes and he have just agreed to this latter claim. Cebes' comment, however, suggests a lack of confidence in their agreement as an indication of the actual truth of the claim. That another argument for it now follows likewise indicates that the claim that the living come to be from the dead is not regarded as securely grounded. Yet Socrates prefaces the third cyclical argument by remarking that he and Cebes have not been wrong to agree that the living come to be from the dead (οὐδ' ἀδίκως ὡμολογήκαμεν, ὡς ἐμοὶ δοκεῖ, 72a11–12). One needs to be careful about this claim. One should not suppose that Socrates is being made to endorse all the premises and inferences of the first two arguments. Instead, he seems to be suggesting that their agreement that the living come to be from the dead and thus that the souls of the dead continue to exist is not misplaced *despite* the fact that the antecedent claim is as yet inadequately grounded. One can in fact be right in believing a claim, when it is true, even in cases where the grounds for one's belief do not properly justify it. Some such sentiment appears to underwrite Socrates' remark here. The question remains, however, how Socrates can be confident that Cebes has not been wrong to agree that the living come to be from the dead. It may seem that Plato is representing Socrates as knowing what he needs to know to be confident about the fate of the soul, and thus confident in the face of death, and likewise as knowing how to lead others to such knowledge. We shall return to the question of whether this is so after considering the progress made in the remaining arguments.

6 The Recollection Argument's Introduction of the Forms Hypothesis

The transition to the recollection argument is made immediately by Cebes himself, who states that the cyclical arguments' conclusions are also entailed by Socrates' theory that learning is recollection (72e3–73a3). Cebes' remarks here serve to introduce a fresh antecedent demonstrandum, from which would follow both of the principal demonstranda introduced by his objection at 70b1–4: that the soul exists before birth and that it is capable of understanding when separated from the body. Cebes focuses explicitly on the first of these points when he says that if Socrates' theory that learning is recollection is correct, then our souls must have existed somewhere before their embodiment at birth (72e3–73a3). Socrates develops the argument suggested by Cebes' remarks in conversation with Simmias. This much-discussed argument[32] appears intended to provide better reasons for accepting that learning is essentially recollection than had been offered in the *Meno* (cf. 73b3–4). It focuses on establishing the newly identified antecedent condition for demonstrating the soul's existence prior to birth, namely that learning (or, more specifically, the apprehension of Forms) essentially involves retrieving from latency the knowledge of Forms that belonged to the soul before birth. The argument for the antecedent condition depends on yet another condition antecedent to it, namely the existence of Forms. Thus identification of the theory of recollection as a hypothesis which, if secured, would make it possible to demonstrate that our souls must have existed prior to our births and must have possessed their capacities for intelligence and understanding leads in turn to the identification of yet another hypothesis which, if secured, would make it possible to demonstrate this first hypothesis: our souls must have existed and possessed intelligence prior to birth *if* learning essentially involves recollection, and learning essentially involves recollection *if* there are intelligible Forms. The recollection argument thus leads up to what Socrates will come to identify as his favored hypothesis: the existence of intelligible Forms (100b4–7).[33]

No supporting reason is given for the hypothesis that functions as the argument's first premise – that there is an equal (τι . . . ἴσον), the Equal itself (αὐτὸ τὸ ἴσον), distinct from all the equal things (74a9–12). Simmias simply agrees with Socrates that "we" say there is such a thing as the Equal itself (74b1, cf. 65d4–8). Later in the dialogue Simmias will refer to the existence of Forms as the "worthy hypothesis" on the basis of which he accepted that learning is recollection (92d6–e2). Given the hypothetical standing of the recollection argument's lead premise, Socrates is quite deliberate about calling attention to the conditional status of its conclusion. At the end of the argument he says that *if* there are entities such as the Beautiful and the Good that "we" are always talking about (εἰ μὲν ἔστιν ἃ θρυλοῦμεν ἀεί) and to which we compare all that comes from the senses so as to rediscover what once was ours, *then* our souls must have existed before birth, whereas *if there are no such entities* (εἰ δὲ μὴ

---

[32] Its importance for understanding the metaphysics and epistemology of Forms coupled with the obscurity of certain details has made this the most discussed argument in the *Phaedo*. The focus of the present discussion is on how the argument functions in the dialectical progression of the dialogue. For more detailed treatments of the argument and its problems, see, for example, Ackrill 1973, Morgan 1984, Franklin 2005, Sedley 2006, and Svavarsson 2009.

[33] The *Meno*'s elaboration and defense of the claim that learning essentially involves the recollection of latent knowledge did not depend on the Forms hypothesis, which does not figure in that dialogue.

ἔστι ταῦτα), *then* the argument has been in vain (76d7–e5). This clear statement draws attention to the fact that the argument's lead premise remains a hypothesis unsupported within the argument itself and that the conclusion must accordingly remain provisional until the Forms' existence is properly secured as more than a hypothesis.[34] Socrates then more plainly restates the conclusion's conditional status: "So is this how things stand? It is indeed equally necessary both that these entities exist and that our souls existed even before we were born, and if these entities do not exist, then neither did they" (76e5–6).

Despite this repeated emphasis on the conditional status of the conclusion, Simmias rushes headlong to endorse it since he is more than willing to accept the hypothesis. "There is nothing so clear to me as this," he says, "that all such things exist as surely as anything can, a Beautiful, a Good, and all the others of which you were speaking just now. And I for one think the point has been *sufficiently demonstrated* (καὶ ἔμοιγε δοκεῖ ἱκανῶς ἀποδέδεικται)" (77a2–5, cf. Cebes at 87a3–4). Plato thus depicts Simmias at this point as accepting as a sufficient proof of the soul's immortality what Socrates has taken pains to indicate should not be taken as such, a situation mirrored in Cebes' response at the culmination of the final argument. Simmias will, of course, soon come to have his doubts. His experience of first rashly endorsing this argument as a sufficient demonstration of the soul's immortality, then later coming to wonder whether the soul might be some sort of attunement of the bodily parts, prompts Socrates' thematically significant remarks on the threat of misology. It might seem nonetheless that the recollection argument provides the makings of a demonstration of the soul's antenatal existence, if only its governing hypothesis could be securely established. There are reasons, though, to be cautious about such a prospect. Even Simmias recognizes that the recollection argument does not satisfy Cebes' earlier demand for a demonstration of the soul's postmortem existence and continued capacity and intelligence since the argument has not shown that one's soul continues to exist once one has died (77b1–9, referring to Cebes' worry at 70a). This concern is echoed by Cebes both here (77c1–5) and once again in his subsequent objection to the recollection argument (86e6–87a5). Although Socrates responds at this point by saying that the soul's existence after death could be demonstrated by combining the recollection argument with the results of the foregoing cyclical arguments (77c6–d5), his recognition that Cebes and Simmias desire a more thorough discussion of the question whether the soul is in fact capable of surviving death

---

[34] Cf. Rowe 1993a, 177–8 *ad* 76e2–5: "S.'s point is no more than that the force of the preceding argument will depend on the truth of the claim that things like 'the beautiful' and 'the good' (i.e. 'forms') exist. In so far as that claim . . . remains unestablished, so too will the pre-existence of the soul."

amounts to a tacit acknowledgment of the inadequacy of the arguments thus far. This is as it should be, for, in addition to the cyclical arguments' notable problems, it is hard to see how the hypothesis of the Forms' existence could be the proper basis for securing the claim that the soul's intellective capacity is indestructible.

The recollection argument functions in accordance with the method of hypothesis that informs the dialogue's broader dialectical progression. The hypothesis that learning is recollection, which Cebes introduces as a basis for arguing that the soul exists prior to birth in the body and that it has some intellective capacity during this time, leads to the introduction of the hypothesis that there are Forms. Cebes begins by noting that our souls must have existed somewhere before birth *if* learning is recollection (72e3–73a3), and Socrates then argues that learning must essentially involve recollection *if* there are intelligible Forms. While the recollection argument is the first of the major series to take the existence of Forms as its hypothesis, there is no attempt to secure or justify reliance on this hypothesis. Furthermore, this first argument on behalf of the soul's immortality to employ the Forms hypothesis does little to fulfill one of the critical functions of the method of hypothesis as introduced in the *Meno*, this being to move toward the understanding of the nature of *x* ultimately required to settle a question as to whether *x* is F. The recollection argument itself, that is to say, does little or nothing to clarify the nature of the soul. Doing so becomes the central task, however, in the ensuing affinity argument and in Socrates' replies to Simmias and Cebes' major objections that follow.

7 The Turn to the Nature of Soul in the Affinity Argument

The existence of intelligible Forms continues to function as the governing hypothesis of the affinity argument. Here, for the first time, the discussion begins to focus on the nature of the soul itself.[35] The basic strategy of this argument is, as Socrates says, to determine what kind of thing is subject to dispersal and destruction, and what kind of thing is not, and then to determine to which class the soul belongs (78b4–9). He begins by obtaining Cebes' agreement to the principles that whatever is composite by nature is subject to dissolution, just insofar as it is composite, and, conversely, that whatever is incomposite is not subject to destruction, just insofar as it is incomposite (78c1–5). He then obtains agreement to the less immediately intuitive principle that whatever is constant and unchanging is likely to be incomposite and,

---

[35] Lorenz 2009, 11, goes so far as to characterize the affinity argument as "[t]he argument [in the *Phaedo*] that sheds most light on what Plato takes the nature of the soul to be."

conversely, whatever is not constant and is subject to change is likely to be composite (78c6–9).[36] In short, whatever is immutable will be incomposite and therefore indestructible, whereas whatever is mutable will be composite and therefore destructible. This initial stage of the discussion thus aims to establish the plausibility of the following two sets of entailments: (i) x is indestructible ↔ x is incomposite ↔ x is immutable, and (ii) x is destructible ↔ x is composite ↔ x is mutable.

Socrates next obtains Cebes' agreement that intelligible Forms are perfectly constant and immutable (78c10–d9), whereas the sensible particulars named after them are subject to constant change (78c10–79a11). This division among two kinds of entity, Socrates suggests, is mirrored in the two parts of ourselves, with the body being more similar and akin to what is sensible, while the soul, being itself invisible, is more like those entities that cannot be apprehended by the senses (79b1–c1). In an attempt to reinforce the affinity of the soul to the intelligible Forms, he says that the soul when inquiring on its own and not by means of the body is best able to approach the pure, eternal, and unchangeable objects to which it is itself naturally akin and that, in doing so, its condition is assimilated to the permanence of its objects in the state called φρόνησις or "wisdom" (79c2–d8). Having obtained Cebes' agreement that the soul is more like and akin to the first class of entities, comprising what is "divine, immortal, intelligible, uniform, indissoluble, and permanently stable" (79d9–80b7), he concludes that the soul should resemble its objects in respect of being "altogether indissoluble, or close to this" (80b9–10).[37]

The affinity argument directly addresses the question of what the soul would have to be like to be indestructible and immortal. A moment's reflection shows that it actually implies that the soul would have to be immaterial and not spatially extended, since according to the argument's principles, every material or spatially extended entity is divisible into parts and therefore composite and destructible. Likewise, in focusing on the soul's cognitive relation to Forms, the argument brings to the fore the soul's distinctive feature as the subject of intentional states. There might even seem to be some plausibility in thinking that the subject of intentional states must resemble its objects in key respects, if understanding is indeed going to involve some form of assimilation of the subject to its objects. Be that as it may, the affinity argument also has some worrisome features. One obvious objection to raise would be that, even if the

---

[36] See Rowe 1993a, 182 ad loc., for a good discussion of why these principles are appropriately marked as merely "likely" (εἰκός).

[37] Betegh 2018, 122, recognizes that with the qualification ἢ ἐγγύς τι τούτου, Socrates himself acknowledges that this has not been a conclusive proof. "Indeed," Betegh asks, "what does it mean that the soul is 'nearly' incapable of being disintegrated?"

soul does have a number of features in common with the unchanging, incomposite, and therefore indestructible (and immaterial) Forms, it hardly follows that it shares all these features with them. Of course, this is just to object that the affinity argument is an argument from analogy and as such hardly conclusive. More worrisome is the fact that the very exercise of the soul's characteristic cognitive capacities apparently involves it in various forms of change. This problem likewise relates to the soul's characteristic directive capacity that will be highlighted in Socrates' reply to Simmias' objection that the soul might be an attunement of the bodily parts. There Socrates argues that the soul cannot be an attunement since it is capable of governing the individual and of opposing and controlling the bodily impulses (94b4–95a3). The affinity argument and the reply to Simmias thus identify the soul as the principle of, respectively, intentionality and agency.

The worry that the soul necessarily changes in exercising its distinctive cognitive and directive capacities brings us to one of the hard problems for an understanding of Plato's view of the soul. He is right to identify the soul as the principle of human intentionality and agency, for it has no more characteristic and fundamental functions in humans than operating as the subject of understanding and the governing source of actions. But how can the soul not be subject to change, as the affinity argument strongly indicates he thinks it must not be in order to be indestructible, and yet be the source, seat, or subject of intentionality and agency? One might also suppose there to be a strong prima facie tension between the requirement that the soul be unchanging, if it is to be indestructible, and the specification of its essence in the *Phaedrus* (and *Laws* 10) as a self-mover. One cannot simply respond that the soul is an *unmoved* mover, given how the *Phaedrus* argument at numerous points certainly seems to characterize the soul as moving itself as well as being a source of movement in other things.

Faced with this hard problem regarding Plato's view of the soul, one might be tempted to say that Plato does not mean to insist on the affinity argument's stringent entailments, so that the soul could be indestructible yet still mutable and even, perhaps, composite. Plato in fact appears to introduce just such a possibility in *Republic* 10, immediately after the argument there on behalf of the soul's immortality. The passage is, in several respects, reminiscent of the *Phaedo*'s affinity argument:

> It isn't easy for anything composed of many parts to be immortal if it isn't put together in the finest way, yet this is how the soul now appeared to us [*sc.* composite]. ... Yet our recent argument and others as well compel us to believe that the soul *is* immortal. But to see the soul as it is in truth, we must not study it as it is while it is maimed by its association with the body and

other evils – which is what we were doing earlier – but as it is in its pure
state. . . . We must realize what it grasps and longs to associate with, because it
is inherently related (ὡς συγγενὴς οὖσα) to the divine and immortal and what
always is, and we must realize what it would *become* (οἷα ἂν γένοιτο) if it
followed this longing with its whole being. . . . Then we'd see what its true
nature is and be able to determine whether it has many parts or just one and
whether or in what manner it is put together. (*R.* 10.611b5–612a4, trans.
Grube)

If one were to engage in the speculation this tantalizing passage invites, one
would pursue its promptings to concentrate on the soul's relation to the Forms in
understanding so as to envision what the soul would become if it were fully to
pursue its desire to apprehend what always is and associate with what is itself
divine and indestructible.

There are already intimations within the *Phaedo* itself that the soul's apprehension of the eternal and immutable Forms involves an assimilation whereby it
achieves a permanence of its own. This can be seen in the affinity argument's
fuller description of the soul's condition of φρόνησις or wisdom:

When, though, the soul inquires on its own, it goes there to what is pure, ever
being, deathless, and permanent, and given its natural kinship with it, it *comes
to be* ever with it (ὡς συγγενὴς οὖσα αὐτοῦ ἀεὶ μετ' ἐκείνου τε γίγνεται),
whenever it has come to be by itself and it is possible for it to do so, and it both
ceases its wandering and regarding those things it persists ever in the same
condition, since it apprehends entities of the same sort. Is this not the
condition of the soul that is called wisdom? (*Phd.* 79d1–7, cf. 66a1–6,
67a2–b2)[38]

There is a virtually identical emphasis here and in the *Republic* passage on the
soul's natural kinship with what always is, and there is likewise the same
intimation that the soul is capable of *becoming* immortal through its association
with, and apprehension of, what always is. The idea seems to be that the soul
comes to achieve a limited degree of immortality insofar as its apprehension of
entities that permanently and immutably are what they are involves an assimilation of the soul to these entities whereby part of the soul itself becomes
permanent and immutable. The immortality envisioned here is apparently
restricted to the part of the soul that does not depend on association with the

---

[38] There are echoes here of the earlier descriptions of the soul's freeing itself from its association
with the body so as to operate αὐτὴ καθ' αὑτήν or "on its own" (65a9–c10) and, again, of how
that person will be best prepared to apprehend the nature of each Form who employs the intellect
(διάνοια) itself "on its own and uncorrupted" (66a1–3), which is to say, freed as far as possible
from bodily association such as it necessarily experiences in perception and likewise from the
disturbances and distractions caused by pleasures and pains it experiences as a result of this
association. Wisdom (φρόνησις) here is the excellent condition of the soul when it has engaged
well in the proper activity of this intellect.

body for its functioning, namely the intellect, and the assimilation to what is unchanging and eternal here described would appear to be the same for all souls experiencing it. One might also want to say that the affinity argument's suggestion of how the soul is capable of achieving this degree of immortality forms the proper complement to the recollection argument's account of the soul's existence prior to its embodiment. For the earlier argument suggests that the soul's ability to apprehend the Forms in what we call "learning" is a function of their already existing in latency within the soul. Its "becoming" immortal in assimilating itself to the eternal and unchanging Forms may thus be viewed as a special kind of change wherein the soul, returning to its natural state, becomes what it, in some real sense, already was. The soul might therefore be capable of changing in this way without transgressing the set of entailments specified at the outset of the affinity argument.

These speculations involve pursuing lines of thought suggested by the affinity argument.[39] They are presented here to suggest that although this argument is certainly no proof of the soul's immortality – it is, after all, an argument from analogy – it both focuses the discussion in a philosophically admirable manner on what the soul would have to be like in order to be indestructible and then goes some distance toward suggesting how it might, in some way and to some degree, actually be such as to fulfill these stringent requirements. Whatever type of response to the hard problem it may be suggesting, it remains the case that, within the *Phaedo*'s dialectical progression, the affinity argument plays the role of shifting the discussion to the nature of the soul itself. It proves less informative about this crucial topic than it might because it asks not what the soul essentially is, but what it is like or resembles. While this is not an unrevealing avenue of inquiry, it is less direct than what we will find in the final argument. Thus it should be no surprise that Plato has Socrates, after the end of the affinity argument, emphasize that "there are still many doubtful points and many available objections, at least if anyone wants a thorough discussion of these matters" (84c6–7). For one thing, the argument's governing hypothesis still awaits the more adequate articulation Socrates will provide in his intellectual autobiography. Most importantly, again, an actual attempt at a proof of whether the soul has the attribute of immortality is going to require a specification of what the soul itself essentially is.

---

[39] Compare how Betegh 2018 sees a different set of problems emerging from the affinity argument ultimately addressed in the *Timaeus'* conception of the cosmic soul and its relation to individual human souls. Within the *Phaedo* itself Betegh sees the affinity argument as reformulating some of the central themes of Socrates' defense of the philosophical life regarding the soul's relation to the body, even though it leaves the precise nature of the soul's affinity to the Forms underspecified (Betegh 2018, 122–5).

8 Soul as Substance in Socrates' Response to Simmias

Equipped with his more adequately formulated hypothesis, Socrates will try to make some progress toward such a specification in the dialogue's final argument that is part of his response to Cebes' objection. Progress is also made toward understanding what soul is in Socrates' response to Simmias' objection that it might be some sort of *harmonia* or attunement. The affinity argument has approached the question of whether the soul is immortal or indestructible by specifying that anything that is so must be incomposite and immutable and by then considering whether soul might plausibly be thought to have the attributes that would entail its indestructibility. It approaches this further question by hypothesizing the existence of Forms, which have these attributes, and proposing that the kinship of soul to Forms evident in the cognitive relation it has to them suggests that it, too, has the attributes entailing its indestructibility. While the argument carries the dialectic forward by focusing attention on the nature of soul, its approach is problematic because it is considering at best indirectly what the soul itself is, by focusing on one of its principal activities. Simmias' suggestion that the soul is a *harmonia* or attunement is the first (and only) account offered in the dialogue of the soul's own nature. In articulating his objection to the affinity argument, that the attunement of the strings of a lyre might likewise be described as "something invisible, without body, beautiful and divine" while clearly being incapable of surviving the lyre's destruction, he introduces the view that the soul is itself a *harmonia* of the body's elements:

> Indeed, Socrates, I think you must have this in mind, that we really do suppose the soul to be something of this kind; as the body is stretched and held together by the hot and the cold, the dry and the moist, and other such things, our soul is a blending (*krasis*) and *harmonia* of those things when they are mixed with each other rightly and in due measure. (*Phd.* 86b5–c3)

Although this view is sometimes presumed to be Pythagorean, there are reasons to doubt this association.[40] What is important for present purposes is what Socrates' arguments against Simmias' view imply about the soul's nature.

---

[40] Macrobius explicitly states that Pythagoras and Philolaus said the soul was a *harmonia* (*in Somn. Scip.* 1.14.19 = 44A23 DK), and McKirahan 2016 argues that Simmias is presenting Philolaus' view. But Simmias is not, *pace* McKirahan, subscribing to the view here or in any other way indicating that it derives from Philolaus. The words he here uses to introduce it – καὶ γὰρ οὖν, ὦ Σώκρατες, οἶμαι ἔγωγε καὶ αὐτόν σε τοῦτο ἐντεθυμῆσθαι – show that he is instead speculating that Socrates has in mind such a view of the soul. One can see why he might do so from the way Aristotle treats this same theory in *On the Soul* 1.4, not as a theory of the Pythagoreans (whose views on the soul he has already cited earlier in the chapter at 404a16–20 and 407b21–4), but as a generally popular idea: "There is yet another opinion about soul, which has commended itself to many as no less probable than any of those we have hitherto mentioned, and has rendered public account of itself in the court of popular discussion. Its supporters say that the soul is a kind

Socrates first argues that since no soul is more or less a soul than another (93b4–7), then, if the soul is an attunement, no soul will be more or less attuned than another (93d1–e3). On the assumption that good souls display attunement while bad souls lack attunement (93c3–10), he argues that all the souls of all living creatures are equally good (94a8–11). Since this conclusion conflicts with the common view, which both Socrates and Simmias accept, that some souls are good while others are bad (93b8–c1), they see that they must reject the view that the soul is an attunement (94a12–b3). Socrates introduces the idea that good souls display *harmonia* by asking whether those who say the soul is a *harmonia* will say that a good soul has yet another *harmonia*. His point is in effect that to identify the soul itself as a *harmonia* amounts to a category mistake: *harmonia* is not the nature of soul but belongs to soul as its good-making attribute. The point that no soul is more or less a soul than another likewise points to the view that soul is a substance rather than a quality or attribute of a substance, as a *harmonia* is. Substance, Aristotle will say in the *Categories*, does not admit of a more and a less, in the sense that no given substance is more or less a substance than another substance of its kind or than itself at another time (Arist. *Cat.* 5.3^{b}34–4^{a}9). Qualities, by contrast, do admit of being more and less (Arist. *Cat.* 8.10^{a}26–11^{a}4).[41] The slight anachronism of putting the point in Aristotelian terms can be avoided if one simply says that Socrates' point that no soul is more or less a soul than another – that is, that souls do not vary in degree – marks the

---

of harmony; for harmony is a blend (*krasis*) or composition (*sunthesis*) of contraries, and the body is compounded out of contraries" (*de An.* I 4.407^{b}27–32, trans. Smith). That Aristotle has in view the theory Simmias advances in the *Phaedo* is suggested by the similarity, extending to verbal echoes, between Simmias' articulation and Aristotle's own presentation. Thus when Simmias says he thinks Socrates must have in mind that "we" suppose the soul is a *harmonia*, the "we" will refer to people generally, not to "we Pythagoreans." Clearly, Aristotle's evidence must be given precedence over that of a late author such as Macrobius. The most obvious obstacle to attributing the *harmonia* theory to the Pythagoreans, however, is that it is flatly incompatible with the Pythagorean doctrine of the soul's immortality, as Simmias' own objection effectively points out. Cf. Hackforth 1952, 102–3, Gallop 1975, 148, Rowe 1993a, 204 ad loc., and the discussion of Macrobius' testimonium in relation to the evidence in the *Phaedo* and Aristotle at Huffman 1993, 323–32.

[41] The distinction between substance and quality is likewise at issue in an attempted *reductio* of Plato's argument attributed to Epicurus by Philoponus: "The sweet admits of more and less. But honey does not admit of more and less for it is a substance. Then honey is not sweet – which is absurd" (τὸ γλυκύ, φησί, τὸ μᾶλλον καὶ ἧττον ἐπιδέχεται, τὸ μέλι τὸ μᾶλλον καὶ ἧττον οὐκ ἐπιδέχεται· οὐσία γάρ ἐστι· τὸ μέλι ἄρα οὐκ ἔστι γλυκύ, ὅπερ ἄτοπον) (Epicur. *ap.* Phlp. *in de An.* 143.3–6 Hayduck). Philoponus' criticism that the argument fails to isolate the respects in which "the sweet" and honey admit of more and less, so that the conclusion does not follow, is a somewhat convoluted way of making the point that Epicurus fails to attend properly to the distinction (143.17–31). Gottschalk 1971, 196–8, first draws attention to this argument; Warren 2006 provides detailed discussion of Epicurus' argument and its apparent dialectical context, Philoponus' criticisms, and echoes in Lucretius. Philoponus elsewhere records that Aristotle in the *Eudemus* argued against the attunement theory on the grounds that attunement has a contrary but the soul has no contrary (Phlp. *in de An.* 141.24–5 Hayduck = Arist. frag. 45 Rose^3).

soul as a different type of entity than an attunement, which is subject to such variation. His point that attunement is not what soul is but belongs to soul as its good-making attribute marks the soul as a more fundamental entity.

Socrates' second argument focuses on another difference between the soul and an attunement and in doing so highlights a crucial characteristic of the soul already, though less directly, highlighted in the affinity argument itself. Unlike an attunement, Socrates says, which can neither be in a state other than that of its components nor act or be acted upon in any way different than those components, the soul is capable of controlling and opposing the bodily feelings, and thus the soul cannot be an attunement (premises at 92e4–93a10, argument at 94b4–95a3). This argument emphasizes how the soul is the principle of agency, as opposed to the merely reactive behavior associated in the *Phaedo* with the body. Already in the affinity argument soul has been likened to the divine insofar as the capacity to rule and govern is characteristic of both (79e8–80a5). Socrates' second argument against Simmias' attunement theory brings this characteristic of the soul to the fore.[42]

9 Toward the Nature of Soul in the Final Argument

In responding to Cebes' objection that the soul might survive the deaths of several individuals and be reincarnated numerous times without necessarily being immortal and imperishable (86e6–88b8, recapped by Socrates at 95b8–e4), Socrates indicates that a response will require a general examination of the causes of generation and destruction (95e9–96a1). He describes his long-standing interest in the factors responsible for things' changes and character and how he ultimately turned to conceptual theorizing governed by the assumption that there are Forms. He explains how appeal to these entities enabled him to overcome the confusion he found himself experiencing in trying to account for apparently simple states of affairs, and his explanation suggests how best to understand what he here identifies as his favored hypothesis. It suggests that the Form of *F*-ness is the property whose instantiation by *x* is a necessary and

---

[42] See Boys-Stones 2004, 15–16, for the suggestion that this argument invokes the psychological theory of the historical Phaedo in his lost dialogue *Zopyrus*. Sedley 1995, 8–9, developing a suggestion by Myles Burnyeat, had already suggested that Plato chose Phaedo as the *Phaedo*'s narrator because he had stressed in the *Zopyrus* Socrates' ability to overcome the proclivities suggested by his own physiognomy. The evidence for Phaedo's *Zopyrus* is assembled at Rosetti 1980, 183–98, and Giannantoni 1990, 125–6. Included among Rosetti's evidence but surprisingly not among Giannantoni's is the crucial testimonia at Cic. *Tusc.* IV 80: "At one gathering, Zopyrus, who claimed to be able to perceive someone's nature from their physical appearance, inferred that he [Socrates] had many vices. Everyone else, who could not see these vices in Socrates, laughed at him; but Socrates encouraged him by saying that those vices had been implanted in him, but that he had cast them out of himself by reason" (trans. Boys-Stones and Rowe).

sufficient condition of x's being F. Participating in the Form of Beauty is what makes something beautiful, which is to say that it is beautiful in virtue of its instantiation of the beauty-making property or the property that is a necessary and sufficient condition of anything's being beautiful (cf. 100b3–e3). The question of immediate concern is whether the more adequate formulation of the Forms hypothesis enables the final argument to make greater progress toward a specification of what the soul essentially is. Is progress made toward a real definition of soul? In considering this question, it is important to realize first how much of the final argument is devoted to distinguishing various ways in which a subject can have a property. When the dialogue frame intrudes momentarily in the transition to the final argument, Phaedo marks the existence of the Forms as a hypothesis secured for the purpose of the discussion by the participants' mutual agreement before recapping the analysis of predication that it involves. On this analysis, things other than the Forms are said to be what they are by participating in the Forms: τούτων [*sc.* τῶν εἰδῶν] τἆλλα μεταλαμβάνοντα αὐτῶν τούτων τὴν ἐπωνυμίαν ἴσχειν (102b2–3). That is to say, in the case of each x that is not identical with the Form of F-ness, "x is F" is understood as indicating that x participates in the Form of F-ness. In the often odd-sounding discussion between Socrates and Cebes which Phaedo is then made to report, the focus moves beyond this basic model of predication to isolating some of the various types of predication. The purpose is ultimately to distinguish attributes a thing has in virtue of itself from ones it does not, so as eventually to isolate life as an attribute that soul has necessarily.

According to the basic theory, Socrates notes, when one says that Simmias is larger than Socrates and smaller than Phaedo, one means that Simmias has his share of both Largeness and Smallness (102b3–6). Moving beyond the basic semantic analysis, he also notes that these statements are misleading if taken to imply that Simmias is larger than Socrates and smaller than Phaedo *in virtue of being Simmias*: "For, surely, it's not Simmias's nature to be taller than Socrates, due to being Simmias, but rather due to the tallness he happens to have" (102c1–3). This is tantamount to saying that the statements under consideration are to be understood as indicating Simmias' possession of an accidental attribute, for such an attribute is precisely one that a thing possesses, though not in virtue of its nature. It would in fact be compatible with Simmias being Simmias for Simmias not to be taller than Socrates. Plato marks the relevant distinction by use of the dative case to indicate just what it is (or is not) in virtue of that Simmias has the attribute of being larger than Socrates: it is not part of his nature to have this attribute, or by virtue of being Simmias that he does so, but by virtue of the largeness he happens to possess (οὐ γάρ που πεφυκέναι Σιμμίαν ὑπερέχειν τούτῳ, τῷ Σιμμίαν εἶναι, ἀλλὰ τῷ μεγέθει ὃ τυγχάνει ἔχων,

102c1–3). The attributes in question happen also to be relative attributes, a further distinction Plato marks by use of the preposition πρός: Simmias is said to be larger than Socrates, not because Socrates is Socrates, but because of the smallness Socrates has *relative to* Simmias' largeness (ὅτι σμικρότητα ἔχει ὁ Σωκράτης πρὸς τὸ ἐκείνου μέγεθος) (102c2–4, cf. c6–8). Thus in saying that Simmias is larger than Socrates, one picks out an attribute of Simmias that is both accidental – that is, an attribute he has, though not just in virtue of being himself – and relative – that is, an attribute he has only in relation to an attribute of some other subject, which in this case turns out also to be an accidental feature of that other subject.

Socrates now proceeds rather laboriously to make the point that, while individual subjects can become, for instance, larger or smaller, these accidents of individuals such as their largeness and smallness cannot themselves "admit" their opposites (102d6–103c2). That is to say, an attribute cannot itself become or admit its own opposite, though the individual possessing that attribute can usually come to possess the opposite attribute. The ensuing treatment of things that, while not themselves opposites, will never admit one of a pair of opposites shifts the focus to cases where a subject has a feature in such a way that it cannot fail to have it while being what it is, or where a subject's failing to have a certain feature is incompatible with its being what it is. Such features, unlike Simmias' tallness relative to Socrates, *will be* ones the subject has in virtue of its nature. The initial cases are those of fire being hot, snow being cold, and three being odd. Thus Socrates expects and obtains Cebes' endorsement of the claim that snow is incapable of accepting the property of being hot and still being just what it was (ὅπερ ἦν), namely snow, while also being hot (103d5–7). In like fashion, fire is incapable of accepting the attribute of being cool and still being just what it was (ὅπερ ἦν), namely fire, while also being cold (103d10–12). Socrates is here isolating a way for an attribute to belong to its subject that is distinct from the way smallness and largeness were just understood to belong to Simmias. Here the attribute belongs to its subject in a non-accidental manner: in addition to the Form of *F*-ness itself being *F*-ness for all eternity, there are also instances where "something else, while it is not that Form, still always possesses its character whenever it exists" (103e4–5). The example of the relation between oddness and the number three clarifies the principle. Not only must the Form of Odd always be designated as Odd but there are also many other things (e.g. the number three) that are not identical with the Odd but that one must call odd, as well as by their own names, in virtue of their being by their very nature such as never to be deprived of the Odd, so long as they exist (103e6–104a4).

In this way Plato has now identified a distinct type of predication in which a property belongs necessarily rather than merely accidentally to its subject.

Here it is critical to observe the distinction between properties that necessarily belong to a subject and properties that would belong in a specification of the subject's essence or what it is to be a thing of that type. Clearly, there is such a distinction to be made, since not every necessary property of a subject will be an essential or defining property of that subject. It is highly relevant that Plato's examples at this point in the final argument are all of necessary, rather than defining or essential, properties. Although fire is necessarily hot and snow necessarily cold, a specification of what it is to be fire or snow would not need to mention these properties.[43] Likewise, while the number three is necessarily odd, one need not mention oddness in specifying what it is to be three. This distinction between necessary and defining properties is not new in the *Phaedo*. It features prominently, for example, in Socrates' explanation of what is wrong with Euthyphro's attempt to specify the nature of piety as what all the gods love: "when asked what piety is, Euthyphro, you apparently were not willing to reveal for me its essence (τὴν ... οὐσίαν ... αὐτοῦ), but only to tell me some attribute (πάθος ... τι) respecting it, that piety has this attribute of being loved by all the gods" (*Euthyphr.* 11a7–b1). Socrates certainly does not deny that what is truly pious will necessarily be loved by all the gods. He merely denies that being loved by all the gods is what it is to be pious. Furthermore, his argument against the proposed specification of the nature of piety as what all the gods love indicates that piety's necessary property of being loved by all the gods is one it will possess in virtue of its nature, whatever that proves to be. For the argument hinges on the point that piety is loved by all the gods *because* it is pious (*Euthyphr.* 10d1–8).

Similarly, in the *Phaedo*'s final argument, the rather deliberate manner in which Plato isolates oddness as a property that must belong to the number three serves, among other things, to suggest that this necessary property of three belongs to the number in virtue of its nature. Thus in the initial clarification of the general principle articulated at 103e2–5 via its application to Oddness and the number three, Socrates says that one must call the number three odd as well as three "in virtue of its being of such a nature (διὰ τὸ οὕτω πεφυκέναι) that it is never deprived of the Odd" (104a2–3). He says again, as he explains the point, that three, five, and half the number series "are naturally such" (οὕτως πέφυκε)

---

[43] Although this distinction is crucial to understanding the final argument, it is hardly noticed in the literature. Politis 2010, 106–7, comes close in suggesting that Plato distinguishes between "things that are essentially f while being distinct from the essence of f" and "the essence of f itself," though he means for the former to be something distinct from being necessarily F. Both Frede 1978, 29, and Frede 2011 characterize the distinction simply as one between essential and accidental properties or qualities (so also, e.g., O'Brien 1967, 200, Bostock 1986, 180). The failure to mark the distinction between necessary and essential properties may in part account for her impulse to construe the final argument as more conclusive than it actually is.

that each is always odd (104a7–8). It remains a further question just what three
is in its nature or essentially such that it is necessarily odd. Nevertheless, the
determination that three is necessarily odd may well be a useful step toward
being able to specify the nature or essence of three. In general, while a property
that *x* has necessarily but not essentially or, to follow Plato's idiom here, *in
virtue of* its nature is distinct from a property that belongs to *x* essentially or *in* its
nature, nevertheless a determination that *F* is a necessary property of *x* may well
constitute progress toward a specification of *x*'s nature or essence.

Socrates concludes the discussion of the preliminary cases by securing
Cebes' agreement to the general analytical principle that "not only does an
opposite not admit its opposite, but also that which introduces a certain opposite
into whatever it itself enters – the introducer will itself never admit the opposite
of what is introduced" (105a2–5). The first part of this principle pertains to
instances of opposites or opposite attributes such as "the largeness in us," which
Socrates said "never admits smallness" but "either retreats and yields its place
whenever the opposite, smallness, advances toward it, or else perishes upon the
opposite's advance" (102d6–e2). The second part of the principle pertains to
those things described just before as compelling whatever they occupy to
possess not only their own character but also always the character of a certain
opposite (104d1–3). These things that invariably compel what they affect to
possess a certain opposite can never themselves take on the opposite attribute
but must likewise either retreat or perish. This general principle provides an
analytical tool for distinguishing necessary from merely accidental attributes;
that is to say, attributes a thing has in virtue of what it is as opposed to attributes
it has in virtue of something else. The principle will now be deployed to show
that life is a necessary attribute of soul.

Socrates' declaration at 100b7–9 that, if granted his favored hypothesis of the
Forms' existence, he hopes to be able to discover (ἀνευρήσειν) that soul is
deathless (ὡς ἀθάνατον ἡ ψυχή) is a fair indication of the final argument's
immediate demonstrandum. Cebes has already prior to this argument shown
himself prone to conflating the soul's being deathless with its being indestructible. In framing his major objection after the initial series of arguments, he said
to Socrates that "anyone who faces death with confidence is senselessly confident if he cannot demonstrate that soul is altogether both deathless and indestructible (ἀθάνατόν τε καὶ ἀνώλεθρον)" (88b3–6). The fact that Socrates
subsequently acknowledges, in recapping Cebes' objection, that he asks for
the soul to be proven both indestructible and deathless (95b9–c1) makes the
absence of any mention of indestructibility at 100b7–9 all the more noticeable.
The restricted thesis that the soul is deathless goes only so far as what the final
argument might in fact be thought to demonstrate. Socrates obtains Cebes'

agreement that the general principle articulated in the preceding discussion applies in the case of the relation between body, soul, and life – that soul always brings life to whatever body it occupies (105c9–d5) – and, therefore, that soul will never itself admit the attribute opposite to life, or death, but is instead deathless (105d6–e7). Socrates pauses here to mark the fact that they have now shown what he said at 100b7–9 he hoped to discover: "Well, then," Socrates says, "should we say that this [*sc.* that soul is deathless] has been shown (ἀποδεδεῖχθαι)? Or what do you think?", to which Cebes replies that this has been shown quite sufficiently (μάλα γε ἱκανῶς) (105e8–9). Socrates has at this point shown as much as he said he hoped to on the basis of his favored hypothesis.

Although he has now fulfilled his stated intention to demonstrate that soul is deathless, Socrates has not lost sight of Cebes' demand that soul be shown to be both deathless *and* indestructible. Plato now has Socrates proceed with an additional argument on behalf of soul's indestructibility (105e10–107a1). Its structure is ultimately simple: $(x)(Fx \rightarrow Gx)$, Fa; Ga – where F is "deathless," G is "indestructible," and a is soul. Whatever is deathless is also indestructible, soul is deathless; therefore, soul is indestructible. The minor premise comes directly from the conclusion of the previous argument, which has shown life to be a necessary attribute of soul. The major premise is much less secure. The preliminary survey of cases – that if what is uneven had to be imperishable, then three would be so, and that if what cannot be hot or what cannot be cold were imperishable, then snow or fire would be so and would retreat (rather than being destroyed) at the onset of heat or cold (105e10–106a11) – serves merely to introduce the major premise while furnishing it little or no support. Nevertheless, it is at this point that Cebes precipitously and illicitly endorses it. Socrates has just articulated the basic structure of the argument and thereby focused the discussion on the status of its major premise: "So now, too, with respect to what is deathless (ἀθάνατον), if it is agreed by us to be also indestructible (ἀνώλεθρον), then in addition to being deathless soul would also be indestructible – but if not, another argument would be needed" (106c9–d1). When Cebes says no further argument is necessary, Socrates does not simply agree but instead provides some further argumentation designed to support the crucial inference of the major premise. This further argumentation, often ignored in reconstructions, takes the form of an argument from analogy: since God and the Form of Life are not only deathless but also are never destroyed, then anything else that is deathless is likewise never destroyed (106d5–7). He concludes by summarizing the basic argument: whatever is deathless is also indestructible, soul is deathless; therefore, soul is indestructible (106e1–3). Although some have wanted to understand this argument as conclusive, Cebes' endorsement of the major premise is evidently hasty, and this additional bit of argument by Socrates can hardly be regarded as securing it.[44]

The proper question to be asked at this point is whether the nature of the soul, in virtue of which it has life as a necessary attribute, is such that the soul must likewise be indestructible.[45] The analysis in the preceding argument has brought the discussion to the point where life has been identified as an attribute soul possesses in virtue of its nature. This identification of an important necessary attribute of soul might well be regarded as progress toward a proper identification of soul's essential nature. In the dialectical progression of the dialogue's arguments, the need to understand the soul's nature or essence in order to determine conclusively whether it is in fact immortal has become ever clearer. The affinity argument and the response to Simmias' objection have focused on the soul as the seat and principle of intentionality and agency. The response to Cebes' objection, however, appears to have progressed to a point from which one could make the intuitive leap required to grasp what soul is essentially.[46] For the result that life is an attribute soul has necessarily or in

---

[44] Frede 1978, 31–2, takes 106d5–7 as pointing to being essentially alive as a common characteristic shared by God, the Form of Life, etc. She then defends the argument via the following reconstruction of its final stage: "if destruction for a living being is its loss of life (death), then deathlessness implies indestructibility. Thus the inference is justified that whatever possesses life as an essential attribute cannot be destructible; for if it cannot admit death it cannot go out of existence at all, and must therefore be indestructible as well." Denyer 2007, 94–5, offers a very similar analysis based on the principle identified by Frede that "whatever is alive, whether it possesses life as an essential property or not, can only pass out of existence by accepting death, by dying." This thought suggests the following *modus tollens* argument, which is at the core of Frede's reconstruction and is articulated more perspicuously by Denyer: if a soul perishes, it comes to be dead, but no soul can come to be dead; therefore, no soul ever perishes. Apart from the fact that it is unclear whether the *Phaedo* actually gives this argument or only the materials for its construction, the argument as reconstructed has some of the same problems as are encountered in the cyclical arguments (perhaps not surprisingly, since Frede's reconstruction centers upon how the final argument supposedly clarifies and modifies the law of opposites on which the cyclical arguments were based). In particular, there is the same problem with casting soul as a subject somehow persisting though the change from being alive to being dead as seen in the first cyclical argument. Certainly, no soul can come to be dead, since life is a necessary property of soul, but a soul's ceasing to exist cannot be construed as *its* coming to have the opposite property. Frede 1978 and Denyer 2007 are representative of attempts to find some sort of legitimacy in the argument's transition from the soul's being ἀθάνατος to its also being ἀνώλεθρος. See O'Brien 2007 for a more roundabout attempt. It should be less tempting to treat the final argument as if it were intended as a proof once it is properly appreciated that life is shown to be a necessary though not an essential attribute of soul.

[45] This question may be prompted by the comparison with God and the Form of Life. For as Dorter 2001, 417, perceptively comments: "In what way are the god and the form of life imperishable? If Socrates means that they are imperishable because they are deathless then he is simply following Cebes in begging the question. Both are deathless and both are imperishable, but they are not imperishable *because* they are deathless."

[46] Cf. Arist. *De an.* I 1.402^{b}15–25: "It seems not only useful for the discovery of the causes of the incidental properties of substances to be acquainted with the essential nature of those

virtue of its nature prompts the further, crucial question: just what is the nature of soul in virtue of which it necessarily has this attribute of life? The dialectical progression of the *Phaedo* in accordance with the method of hypothesis stops just here. Although the responses of Socrates and Simmias to the final argument suggest that the question of the soul's immortality has not been settled and that further argument and discussion are in fact needed, no further progress is made in this dialogue.[47]

Elsewhere, of course, Plato does provide an answer to the crucial question as to the nature of soul. Both the *Phaedrus* and the *Laws* specify being a self-mover as the soul's nature or essence.[48] This specification of the soul's nature would provide an answer to the question that has come into focus in the *Phaedo*'s final argument. The essence of soul is self-motion, namely the ability to initiate by itself change in itself and in other things, and whatever is essentially a self-mover has life as a necessary attribute; therefore, soul has life as a necessary attribute. This specification of the soul's nature also provides the requisite basis for answering the question as to whether soul is not only deathless in this limited sense but indestructible as well. Plato's answer comes in the argument for the soul's immortality at *Phaedrus* 245c–246a, where he argues that whatever is ever-moving[49] is immortal, and any self-mover never ceases moving and is thus ever-moving, so that any self-mover is immortal, but every soul is essentially a self-mover, and so every soul is immortal. This argument for the soul's immortality is superior to any of the arguments given in the *Phaedo*, precisely because it proceeds deductively from a specification of the nature or essence of soul. When one understands what soul is in its nature or essentially, then one is in the best position to determine whether it is or is not immortal. The *Phaedrus* argument thus is not based upon a hypothesis but proceeds directly from this understanding as a first principle. The interlocutors of the *Phaedo*, however, resemble Socrates and Meno in seeking to determine whether something has a certain attribute when they do not as yet know the nature of that thing or what it

---

substances ... but also conversely, for the knowledge of the essential nature of a substance is largely promoted by an acquaintance with its properties: for, when we are able to give an account conformable to experience of all or most of the properties of a substance, we shall be in the most favourable position to say something worth saying about the essential nature of that subject" (trans. Smith).

[47] Frede 1978, 39, reproaches Plato for leaving the nature of the soul undefined in the *Phaedo* since she regards this as a violation of the rule that one ought not to argue that *x* has a certain quality before identifying the nature of *x* itself (for which she cites *M.* 100b, *R.* 1.354c–e, *Euthyphr.* 15d, and *La.* 199c ff.). It has been argued here, of course, that this rule and the method of hypothesis introduced in service of it have been governing the dialogue's arguments from the start.

[48] *Phdr.* 245e2–4, *Leg.* 10.895e10–896a1; cf. *Ti.* 46d5–e2.

[49] For reasons to prefer the majority manuscript reading ἀεικίνητον over αὐτοκίνητον in Oxyrhynchus papyrus 101, see Decleva Caizzi 1970 and Bett 1986, 4 n. 6.

is essentially. Socrates, Cebes, and Simmias must therefore proceed analytically toward what they would need to know to settle the issue, and by means of the method of hypothesis that is the proper heuristic device for those in their situation. Although the *Phaedo*'s arguments prove inconclusive, they serve Plato's purpose of leading his readers toward apprehending for themselves what he believes they need to apprehend to know that the soul is immortal.

10 Justified Belief on the Way to First Principles

Aristotle famously reports how Plato used to ask whether we are proceeding from the ἀρχαί or to the ἀρχαί (Arist. *EN* I 4.1095ᵃ32–3). Anyone who would criticize the *Phaedo*'s arguments for their failure as deductively valid proofs of the soul's immortality should be reminded of Plato's question. The dialectical progression of the dialogue, proceeding in accordance with the method of hypothesis, leads deliberately toward a point where one would know whether the soul is immortal in virtue of being able to provide a sound deductive argument, the premises of which would include a specification of the essential nature of the soul itself. Socrates and his interlocutors do not reach this point in the dialogue. Socrates is nonetheless described by Phaedo in the *Phaedo*'s opening frame as having been happy (εὐδαίμων) as he died nobly and without fear (*Phd.* 58e3–4). Phaedo's early description is brilliantly borne out at the end of the dialogue by Plato's portrayal of Socrates' serenity as he drinks the hemlock and dies without disturbance. His calm demeanor might appear awkward, given Cebes' earlier comment that anyone facing death with confidence is foolishly confident unless he can show that soul is altogether both deathless and indestructible (88b3–6, recapped by Socrates at 95b8–e2). Socrates has not demonstrated that soul is both deathless and indestructible. Surely, though, one is not supposed to regard Socrates' serenity at the end as foolish.

Cebes' remark might seem grounds for supposing that the final argument does, in fact, demonstrate that the soul is both deathless and indestructible. Such a supposition, though, would require discounting the numerous indications that Socrates himself does not regard even this argument as conclusive, including the care he takes to distinguish the relevant senses of ἀθάνατος in the argument's final stages, his approbation of Simmias' lingering doubts, and his indication of the need for a still clearer examination of the initial hypotheses (107b4–6). Alternatively, one might suppose that we are to imagine Socrates capable of demonstrating that soul is both deathless and indestructible even though he does not do so here.[50] His response to Simmias' lingering doubts might seem to suggest that this is the case: "And if you analyze these [*sc.* the

---

[50] An interpretation along these lines is developed at Kanayama 2000, 86–100.

initial hypotheses] sufficiently," he tells Simmias, "you will, so I think, follow the reasoning as far as it is possible for a human being to pursue it – and if this result becomes clear, you will inquire no further" (107b6–9). One might wonder how Socrates can be made to offer this assurance unless he is meant to know already what will result from this further analysis. More generally, one might suppose that we are to understand Socrates' ability to lead Cebes and Simmias as he does – from the opening discussion of the prohibition against suicide, through the initial series of arguments on behalf of the soul's immortality, to the response to their objections, and apparently to the verge of an actual demonstration that soul is both deathless and indestructible – as depending on his own clear understanding of the fundamental premises from which such a demonstration would proceed.[51]

The notion that Socrates is supposed to know how to demonstrate the soul's immortality, even if he does not do so in the course of his discussion with Cebes and Simmias, might appear to account for the confidence Socrates expresses in the conclusions of arguments he understands are inconclusive. We have already noted how he prefaces the third cyclical argument with the remark that he and Cebes have not been wrong to agree that the living come to be from the dead despite its evidently inadequate grounding of the claim. Likewise, at the end of the final argument, Socrates is made to deploy a set of analogies to bolster Cebes' confidence that whatever is deathless is indestructible without, however, endorsing Cebes' misunderstanding of the deathlessness soul has been shown to have in the argument just concluded as equivalent to eternal existence (106d5–7). Socrates' warnings against the dangers of "misology," or distrust in reasoning and argument, might likewise be thought to imply that he has the ability to demonstrate the soul's immortality even if he does not do so here. After describing the audience's disappointment upon hearing Simmias' and Cebes' objections after being convinced by the earlier arguments, Phaedo proceeds to describe how Socrates encouraged him not to succumb because of this reversal to the great evil of mistrusting reason and argument themselves.[52] In particular, Phaedo reports how Socrates said it would be deeply regrettable if the experience of finding flaws in arguments that formerly seemed sound were to turn

---

[51] Plato represents Socrates in this dialogue as resembling Theseus in his ability to lead his companions to safety. Such is the thematic significance of Phaedo's description of Theseus' voyage to Crete, the Athenians' commemoration of which delays Socrates' execution (58a10–b1). The "twice seven" whom Phaedo notes Theseus saved even as he saved himself are mirrored in the fourteen individuals Phaedo names soon after, in two groups of seven, when asked by Echecrates who was present with Socrates on his last day (59b5–c2). Socrates will prove a heroic figure, a latter-day Theseus, in saving his companions as well as himself from the terrors of death. (Cf. Phaedo's heroizing portrayal of Socrates and comparison of him to Heracles at 89a–c.)

[52] Sedley 1995, 14, finds it significant that Socrates addresses his remarks on misology to Phaedo: "he is covertly talking *about* Simmias and Cebes."

a person into a misologist when there was a true and secure argument for him to grasp (90c8–d7). One should acknowledge instead, Socrates says, that the experience is due to one's own lack of skill in argument and thus work at acquiring the requisite dialectical prowess (90d9–e3). This is a clear enough indication that at least the initial series of arguments are meant to be "dialectical" in the sense of promoting development of the skills Socrates here indicates one needs to become a philosopher. More relevantly, however, his reference to the existence of a true and secure argument, even if it is part of a conditional, might be thought to indicate that he is supposed to know of such an argument.

Other thematically significant passages in the dialogue, however, make it difficult to sustain the notion that Socrates is to be regarded as himself having the clear understanding and knowledge toward which he is leading his interlocutors. While Plato may have regarded himself as having the knowledge in question and consequently as able to lead his readers toward understanding for themselves the nature of soul and why it is to be regarded as immortal, there are numerous indications in the dialogue that he does not mean to ascribe this knowledge to Socrates. One such indication comes in the passage that rounds off his admonition to Phaedo against misology, in which Socrates rather remarkably describes himself as not maintaining a properly philosophical attitude. In facing his own death, he says, he runs the risk of not maintaining the disposition of one who loves wisdom (οὐ φιλοσόφως ἔχειν) and of behaving instead like those without proper dialectical training who simply love winning (φιλονίκως); at present he differs from these eristics, he says, who disregard the actual facts of the matter and are intent only on getting the audience to accept their claims, in that he is only incidentally concerned with getting his audience to believe what he says and much more intent on believing himself that what he's saying is so (91a1–b1). Socrates is not one who lacks proper dialectical training. It is in virtue of his dialectical skill that, unlike Phaedo and those whose initial trust was disappointed, he understood that none of the preceding arguments on behalf of the soul's immortality were sound. He apparently also lacks clear knowledge of the soul's immortality; for he would not describe his attitude as he does here if he regarded himself as possessing it. The attitude he is made to ascribe to himself is complex and delicately balanced, for in the comparison he figures as an analogue of both the eristic disputant and the audience to be persuaded. Since he portrays the eristic as intent on getting his audience to believe his claim regardless of its truth, Socrates might seem to be welcoming some form of self-deception. One should not, however, regard Socrates as like the eristics in simply disregarding the actual facts of the matter. His relation to the truth in this instance is subtler, in that, while very much concerned with the truth regarding the fate of his soul, he can appreciate that he is as yet not in a position to provide the kind of justification he would himself regard as secure. This is the epistemic position of one who is arguing to, rather than from, first principles. Socrates expands on the reasoning behind his perhaps unphilosophical attitude by explaining that, if what he says about the soul's immortality should happen to be true, then it is good to be persuaded of it, whereas, if death is really the end, the mistaken belief to the contrary will at any rate have beneficial practical consequences while he's still alive (91b1–7). The question is how someone like Socrates can come to believe that the soul is immortal while appreciating full well that he is not yet able to provide true and secure justification for this belief.

With this question it should begin to be apparent that, with respect to his epistemic situation, the Socrates of the *Phaedo* is not so very different from the figure in dialogues typically considered more purely "Socratic." For Socrates is typically in the position of acknowledging his lack of knowledge at the same time as he is prepared to embrace and defend a number of substantive ethical claims. In the *Apology*, for instance, where his confession of his own ignorance features quite prominently, he alludes to the paradoxical claim that no one does wrong willingly, saying, "I am convinced that I never willingly wrong anyone, but I am not convincing you of this, for we have talked together but a short time. If it were the law with us, as it is elsewhere, that a trial for life should not last one but many days, you would be convinced" (*Ap.* 37a5–b1, trans. Grube). He argues at length on behalf of the claim in the *Gorgias*, and it is in this dialogue that one finds the comment by Socrates that provides perhaps the best perspective on how his profession of ignorance is to be reconciled with his advocacy of certain definite claims. "My position is always the same," he says, "that I do not know in what way these things are so (ταῦτα οὐκ οἶδα ὅπως ἔχει), but that among the people I've met, just as I have here, no one could speak to the contrary without coming off ridiculous" (*G.* 509a4–7). That is to say, he recognizes that he is unable to give an adequate explanation of precisely why the claims he has been advocating are true, and yet it has been his experience that these claims have a certain dialectical impregnability, in that no one he has come across has been able to maintain the contrary without falling into self-contradiction.[53] He considers himself as yet unable to provide adequate grounding or explanation of what makes his claims true, apparently because he regards

---

[53] This remark follows immediately after the comment on the earlier elenctic argument against Polus' claim that suffering wrong is worse than doing wrong (*G.* 474c–475e). Socrates emphatically states that any wrongs done to him or his family are both worse and more shameful for the wrongdoer than the wronged (*G.* 508d–e) and then says that this point has been made evident in his earlier argument with Polus and "is held firm and bound . . . by reasons of iron and adamant, or at least it would seem to be so, which if you, or one still more impetuous than yourself, do not undo, it will not be possible to speak well while saying anything to the contrary of what I am now

himself as having an as yet inadequate grasp of the relevant basic concepts. Most notably, the claim not to know what the good is is a constant feature of Plato's representation of Socrates, and properly justificatory accounts of the practical and ethical claims for which he argues need to be grounded in a clear apprehension of what is good for humans as such. Although he is unable to explain properly why his claims are true, he nevertheless feels that sufficient justification for practical purposes has been provided by his interlocutors' inability to maintain the contrary consistently.

One can in fact be correct in believing a claim, even in cases where the grounds for one's belief do not make that belief indefeasible, when that claim is true. Absent the deductive explanation from the relevant first principles that would be properly justificatory, Socrates contents himself with a justification appropriate for one still relying on hypotheses. Although this does not enable him to explain why things are so, it nevertheless provides him with some genuine assurance that they are so, and for practical purposes, he understands, true belief is as effective a guide as knowledge. He makes this point in the *Meno* immediately after the application of the newly introduced method of hypothesis to the question of whether excellence of character is something that can be taught. There he means it to defuse the objection in the argument against excellence being a kind of knowledge that there have been some notable individuals of excellent character whose excellence seems not to have been based on knowledge. In Plato's representation, Socrates is himself one such individual. The excellence of his behavior during his life has not been grounded in knowledge of what is good for humans as such and thus not in the knowledge that he believes constitutes genuine excellence. Likewise, the excellence of his behavior at the end of his life is not rooted in knowledge of the soul's essential nature and thus not in any clear apprehension of its immortality. Still, Socrates' belief in the soul's immortality is hardly without justification. He has the kind of justification available to one still considering the question of the soul's immortality on the basis of hypotheses. Simmias appears to strike the right note in saying, "On these matters, I think, Socrates, as perhaps you do too, that clear knowledge in this life is either impossible or something very difficult. ... One must accomplish one of these things: either learn or discover whatever the case

---

saying" (*G*. 508e–509a). While this language is strong, it should not be taken to indicate that he regards the elenctic argument against Polus' claim as a proof demonstrating the actual reasons why doing wrong is worse than suffering wrong (presumably, such a proof would have to proceed from a proper understanding of what is good and bad for humans as such). The elenctic argument, instead, by showing that other beliefs Polus has commit him to the contrary of his original claim, does what Socrates here describes: it confirms Socrates' experience of no one being able to maintain the contrary to this claim without coming off ridiculous, which here means falling into contradiction.

may be, or, if this is impossible, sail through life taking the best and most irrefutable of human theories and embarking upon it like a raft" (85c1–d4).[54] While one might hesitate to regard Simmias as adequately expressing Socrates' own perspective, Simmias is nevertheless actually echoing Socrates' earlier description of the attitude of the genuine philosophers' view to the effect that "so long as we have the body, and our soul is suffused with an evil of this sort, we shall never possess sufficiently what we long for, and this thing we say is the truth" (66b5–7). In light of the understanding of the arguments and of Socrates' epistemic attitude developed here, it appears that Simmias' remarks are actually a fair description of how Socrates proceeds in the discussion, as he relies on the hypothesis of the Forms' existence in approaching what he would properly need to understand in order to know whether the soul is in fact immortal; and at the same time Simmias' remarks gesture toward the type of grounding of Socrates' belief that it is immortal that is available to him while he is still relying on hypotheses and proceeding toward a proof that it is so, which would be grounded in a clear understanding of the soul's essential nature.

11 *Mythologia* and the Philosophic Life

Once one sees that the *Phaedo*'s arguments are not intended as proofs of the soul's immortality, it becomes apparent in retrospect that Plato has from early in the dialogue thematized them as arguments of a different order. Consider Socrates' account of why he has been putting to verse fables by Aesop, prefaced by his own proem to Apollo (60c8–61c1). Many times in the past, he says, he dreamt of a figure commanding him: "create art and work at it" (μουσικὴν ποίει καὶ ἐργάζου, 60e6–7). Previously he had thought that in pursuing philosophy he was obeying the order, philosophy being the greatest art (μουσική) (60e7–61a4); but now, in case he interpreted the dream incorrectly, he has taken to composing poems in his cell (61a4–b1). For material he has adopted stories by Aesop because, he says, it is necessary for a poet to make tales (μῦθοι), not arguments (λόγοι), and he is himself no teller of tales – no μυθολογικός (61b2–7). A curious incongruity suggests this self-characterization has thematic significance. When the discussion turns soon after to suicide, Socrates suggests that, since Simmias and Cebes have not heard in detail the views of their master Philolaus on the topic, they ought now

---

[54] Commentators have generally seen Simmias' remarks here as closely resembling Socrates' own accounts of his method. The *communis opinio* is succinctly represented by Rowe 1993a, 202 *ad* 85c2: "The principles which Simmias is about to suggest appear to be identical to S.'s." Sedley 1995, 18–20, while acknowledging that the comparison is apt, suggests that we are meant to recognize that Simmias' and Socrates' interpretations and applications of the method differ because of Simmias' tendency toward misology.

variously "to examine and tell tales about" (διασκοπεῖν τε καὶ μυθολογεῖν, 61e1–2)[55] the afterlife in general. He says this just after noting that he is no μυθολογικός. Then, before setting out his initial arguments for the soul's immortality, he again proposes to "mythologize": Cebes has just said how hard it is for people to believe that when the soul departs the body it still exists somewhere and is not destroyed when a person dies. That the deceased person's soul exists and possesses some power and intelligence, he says, requires no small amount of persuasion (παραμυθίας) and assurance (69e7–70b4). Socrates agrees and asks: "But what, then, should we do? Or would you like us to engage in some speculative discussion (διαμυθολογῶμεν) regarding these matters, as to whether or not things are likely to be so?" (70b6–7). Having previously described himself as no "mythologizer," Socrates nonetheless proposes once again to "mythologize." These uses of the verb (δια)μυθολογεῖν together with the characterization of the ensuing discussion as an effort to determine whether it is likely or not (εἴτε εἰκος οὕτως ἔχειν εἴτε μή, 70b7) that the soul survives apart from the body after death and whether, if so, it still possesses its powers of intelligence – these being, respectively, the major and minor demonstranda emerging from the initial discussion – suggest that Socrates understands that the arguments to come will be something less than proofs.

This is merely one way Plato marks the special status of the dialogue's arguments. Another appears in his instruction to Cebes and Simmias to "sing charms" to the fearful child within who is still afraid of death. After the recollection argument, Simmias expresses the concern he shares with Cebes that even if the argument has shown that the Forms' existence and the soul's antenatal existence are equally necessary,[56] it has not been shown that the soul will exist after death. As Socrates indicates that one could combine the recollection argument with features of the cyclical arguments to construct an argument for this conclusion (77c6–d5), he says Cebes and Simmias still have a "childish fear" (77d7) that the soul will be dispersed at death. When Cebes then asks him to persuade this fearful child within, Socrates says: "You must sing charms (ἐπᾴδειν) to him every day until you charm away (ἐξεπᾴσητε) the fear" (77e8–9). It was once a common understanding of this remark that the charms of myth are required to persuade the irrational element within the soul

---

[55] Rowe 1993a, 125 ad loc., aptly comments that "μυθολογεῖν here either literally means 'telling stories', or, more likely, compares the business of discussion to story-telling."

[56] Simmias' confidence in the Forms' existence leads him to say that he thinks the soul's antenatal existence has been adequately demonstrated (ἔμοιγε ἱκανῶς ἀποδέδεικται, 77a5). This hasty confidence followed by doubt exemplifies the type of experience that potentially leads to the "misology" or distrust of argument Socrates warns against at 89d–90e.

just as arguments are needed to persuade the rational element.[57] But why should Socrates refer to myths in the midst of presenting his *arguments* for immortality? It is more natural, given the context of the reference, to think Socrates is describing his arguments themselves as charms. The characterization is apt if they are not the kind of arguments that yield the security of knowledge but are such that their repetition nevertheless produces a state of the soul that is an adequate guide for appropriate behavior in the face of death.

Socrates employs the image of the charm once more at the conclusion of the dialogue's eschatological myth. After describing what he has come to believe regarding the earth's true nature and the fates that await souls of varying conditions of purity, he says that while it would not be appropriate for a sensible person to insist that things are just as he has related, nevertheless, if the soul is immortal, it is appropriate and worth the risk to believe that something like what he has described is the case – and so one must repeat such things to oneself as charms (καὶ χρὴ τὰ τοιαῦτα ὥσπερ ἐπᾴδειν ἑαυτῷ, 114d6–7). If the elaborate myth of the nature of the underworld and the true earth serves, at one level, to comfort the child within who may still harbor doubts, its principal function is to emphasize the overriding imperative for humans to attend to the care of their souls.[58] Socrates makes this point explicit at both the beginning and again at the end of the myth. After encouraging Simmias to engage in further examination of the hypotheses on which the preceding arguments were based, Socrates introduces his account of the afterlife and the earth's true nature as follows:

> But this, at least, gentlemen, it is right and fitting to bear in mind, that if indeed the soul is immortal,[59] then it requires care not merely for the sake of

---

[57] So Dorter 1982, 8. The notion that Plato's myths are meant to appeal to the irrational part of the soul and his arguments to the rational, which features prominently in, for example, Edelstein 1949, 472–7, is now widely recognized as inadequate.

[58] General studies of his eschatological myths include Annas 1982, Morgan 2000, ch. 7, and Inwood 2009. The studies in Partenie 2009 variously explore the tight connections between myth and philosophy in Plato. On the *Phaedo* myth in particular, see Sedley 1991, Edmonds 2004, ch. 4, Betegh 2006, Pender 2012, and Ebert 2014. Edmonds is particularly insightful on how Plato's myth recasts both traditional themes regarding the soul's journey to the realm of the dead and important ideas from earlier in the dialogue to valorize the philosopher's search for understanding and to advocate anew for the philosophic life.

[59] "if indeed the soul is immortal" = εἴπερ ἡ ψυχὴ ἀθάνατος (107c2). The fact that even after the dialogue's final argument, the thesis of the soul's immortality is marked in this way by Socrates as provisional suggests that ἐπειδὴ ἀθάνατος φαίνεται οὖσα at 107c8 and likewise ἐπείπερ ἀθάνατόν γε ἡ ψυχὴ φαίνεται οὖσα at 114d4 should be taken non-veridically, as "since it appears to be immortal" and "since the soul appears to be immortal," respectively. The translations of these phrases in Gallop 1975, 68–9 – "if a soul *is* immortal" (107c2), "since, in fact, it is evidently immortal" (107c8), and "given that the soul evidently is immortal" (114d4) – strain to give the first phrase a more definite force than it in fact possesses in order to preserve the parallelism with the latter two, apparently on the presumption that φαίνεται οὖσα must be

this time we call "life," but for the sake of all time, and the risk would now really seem to be terrible if one were to neglect it. For if death were a release from everything, it would be a godsend for the wicked to die and to be released simultaneously from their body and from the wickedness in their soul. But now since it appears to be immortal, there would be no other refuge for it from evils or any salvation other than becoming as good and wise as possible. For the soul goes to Hades with no other possessions except its education and upbringing, which are indeed reputed to provide the greatest benefit or harm to the one who has died, right at the outset of its journey to that place. (107c1–d5)

The imperative to care for one's soul so that it may become as good and wise as possible is reminiscent of Socrates' response in the *Apology* to the prospect of being acquitted on the condition that he no longer practice philosophy. Decisively rejecting this condition, he says he will continue to exhort his fellow citizens by asking them whether they are not ashamed of their eagerness to possess inferior goods such as wealth, reputation, and honors, while disregarding the most important things, namely wisdom, truth, and the best possible state of the soul. His divinely ordained service to Athens, he says, consists in endeavoring to persuade young and old alike to care less for their bodies and wealth and more for the best possible condition of their souls (*Ap.* 29d–30b). Here in the *Phaedo* Plato considers the relative value of external or bodily goods and the goods of the soul from the perspective of eternity: if the soul survives the body's demise, then evidently nothing else it may have valued in life will survive with it except its own condition. From the perspective of eternity, then, one ought to strive to make it as good as possible. The myth adds meaning to the idea that the good condition of the soul is in fact something of incomparable value by describing how one's fate in the afterlife depends entirely on the sort of person one was in one's preceding life.

In the course of the myth, Socrates describe the journeys of the pure and impure souls, the true nature of the earth, its brilliant upper regions and those who dwell there, the subterranean streams kept flowing by the powerful pump

---

construed veridically. Compare the renderings of the phrases at 107c8 and 114d4 in Rowe 1993a, ad loc., as "since it is manifestly immortal" and "given that the soul is clearly [something] immortal." While the personal construction φανερός εἰμι followed by a dependent statement with the verb in the participle has a veridical sense (as, e.g., at Hdt. *Hist.* 5.56, 7.18, Isoc. *Orat.* 12.201, Xen. *Mem.* I 1.2, etc.), when φαίνομαι is followed by a supplementary participle in indirect discourse it need not have this veridical sense. See Smyth 1920, §2106 (and §2107), where Pl. *Phd.* 107c8, ἡ ψυχὴ ἀθάνατος φαίνεται οὖσα, is listed alongside examples of the construction with verbs of knowing, learning, remembering, etc. and translated: "it seems that the soul is immortal." Pender 2012, 205–6, acknowledges the conditional sense of all these phrases, on the supposition that Socrates means to be sensitive to Simmias' remaining doubts.

of Tartarus, and the judgment of the different types of souls in Hades. After describing all these things in elaborate detail, he concludes:

> It would not be appropriate for a sensible person to maintain that these things are exactly as I have described them.[60] But that either this or something of this sort is so respecting our souls and their abodes, since the soul appears to be immortal, I do think is appropriate and worth the risk for one who believes it is so – for the risk is a noble one – and one must repeat such things to oneself as charms, which is why I have stretched the story out for so long. For these reasons, then, any man should be confident (θαρρεῖν) regarding the fate of his soul who during his life has dismissed bodily pleasures and adornments as alien and who has regarded them as doing more harm than good, and who has devoted himself to learning and thereby adorned his soul, not with an alien one, but with its own proper adornment of moderation, justice, courage, liberality, and truth, and thus he awaits the journey to Hades and is ready to make the journey whenever fate may summon him. (*Phd.* 114d1–115a3)

In this coda to the myth, Socrates makes explicit the reason for his own confidence in the face of death. Early in the dialogue's opening frame, again, Phaedo had told Echecrates that he found Socrates to be happy (εὐδαίμων) at the end and that he died fearlessly and nobly (58e3–5). He said Socrates had impressed him as one who would have a divine portion in Hades and would fare well (εὖ πράξειν) there if ever anyone did (58e5–59a1). Phaedo subsequently reports how Cebes concluded his objections to the initial series of arguments by saying that, if the soul has been shown to be reborn numerous times and yet has not been shown ultimately imperishable, then anyone who confidently faces death will be foolishly confident (ἀνοήτως θαρρεῖν) unless they are able to show that soul is completely deathless and imperishable (88b3–6). It would be a mistake to take Cebes' comments as representative of Socrates' perspective. For Socrates' own remarks here at the end of the myth indicate that his confidence at the moment of his death is grounded not in any ability to prove decisively that the soul is immortal, but rather in his having lived the best possible life – a life devoted to philosophy and thereby to the proper care of his soul. Socrates had notably mounted his defense of the philosophical life, where he had described philosophy as a preparation for death, in an effort to explain to Simmias and Cebes why, as he says, someone who has devoted his life to philosophy should feel confident (θαρρεῖν) when he is about to die and harbors a hope of attaining great benefits in the world to come (63e8–64a2).[61]

---

[60] Cf. *Phd.* 108d4–e2. At *Gorgias* 523a, Plato has Socrates similarly characterize that dialogue's eschatological myth.

[61] Cf. Annas 1982, 128: "When Socrates prepares to die, he is confident, and this can only be because he takes himself (self-righteously, to our minds) to be the fully good person who can expect rewards" (114d1–115a1). The note of disparagement is unnecessary, as Socrates'

The eschatological myth gives this prospect a detailed vividness while reprising the idea that having lived a life devoted to the proper care of one's soul should make one confident in the face of death.

It is notable that in offering a vision of the benefits awaiting the genuinely philosophical soul, the myth reprises many of the principal themes of the dialogue's earlier defense of the philosophical life. The philosopher, Socrates had said, does not crave physical pleasures or bodily adornments but positively disdains them, and his concern is directed toward the soul, which he endeavors to release as far as possible from its association with the body (64c10–65a8). In pursuing the wisdom he values so highly, the philosopher finds the body a hindrance; he is able to attain the truth he desires only via the activity of reason, which best operates when undistracted by the senses and by pleasure and pain and when it is, again, as free as possible from its association with the body (65a9–d3). In particular, the philosopher is able to apprehend Justice, Beauty, Goodness, and all the other intelligible Forms only with an intellect purified as far as possible from its association with the body (65d4–66a8). The genuine philosophers, he says, acknowledge to one another that "while we possess the body and our soul is contaminated by such an evil, we shall never sufficiently possess what we desire – and we say that is the truth" (66b5–7). Only when we are rid of the body, they say, will we ever know anything purely and attain the wisdom we desire, not while we are alive (66d7–e4). When the god has released us, they say, and we are thus purified and separated from bodily foolishness, it is likely that we will then be among others of the same kind and will have knowledge of all that is pure (67a6–b1). Socrates concludes that there is good reason for one such as himself, whose greatest concern has been with truth and who has thus adequately prepared his soul, to be hopeful that he will finally attain in the afterlife the truth he has desired throughout this life (67b7–c3). The philosophic life Socrates has lived has accordingly been a preparation for death, and it is, again, precisely because he has lived as a philosopher that he is confident and hopeful in the face of death. As he says, "those who pursue philosophy correctly are practicing for death, and dying is least frightening for them of anyone" (67e5–7).

The eschatological myth envisages the philosopher's fulfillment of the desire for the truth to which the soul's embodiment has proved an insurmountable impediment. The myth elaborates upon traditional notions regarding the soul's journey to a place of judgment after death by providing a geographically plausible theory of the regions below and above the portion of the earth familiar

---

confidence is due more particularly to his having devoted his life to philosophy rather than the moral self-righteousness she detects.

to humans as their dwelling-place during their lifetimes.[62] Below this region is the place of judgment and punishment, while above this region is the place Socrates refers to as "the true earth" where good and wise souls are rewarded. There are rewards both for those who have lived exceptionally pious lives and for those whose souls have been purified by philosophy.[63] The exceptionally pious are reborn to dwell on the true surface of the earth, which borders the airy atmosphere as the regions of earth we know border the seas. Although the inhabitants of this true earth above are not without bodies, their cognitive faculties are more acute than ours, largely because they dwell in a purer region: "the sun, moon, and stars are seen by them as they actually are" (111c1–2) because they are able to gaze directly into the ether. The reward for an exceptionally pure life is rebirth to a place where it becomes easier to perfect the understanding (114b6–c2; cf. 111a4–c3). The reward for those adequately purified by philosophy is greater still: emancipated from the cycle of reincarnation, their souls live unembodied for the rest of time, in a place so transcendent that Socrates does not even attempt to describe it (114c2–6). Freed from the body and other earthly impediments, the souls of the philosophers are able to enjoy the apprehension of truth and the objects of the intelligible realm he had so diligently and laboriously pursued throughout his embodied life. This vision of the fate of the genuinely philosophical soul draws not only on the earlier account of the body as a hindrance to the activity of reason but also on the affinity argument's account of the soul as achieving a union with the intelligible objects to which it is akin. When the soul inquires on its own, Socrates had said, "it goes there (ἐκεῖσε οἴχεται) to what is pure, ever being, deathless, and

---

[62] Note λέγεται at 107d5, introducing the idea that the δαίμων assigned each person in life leads their soul to the place of judgment, as well as Socrates' statement at 108a5–6 that his suggestion that the path leading to Hades must have numerous forks and branches is based on the evidence of current rites and practices. The traditional ideas or sources to which Socrates is here gesturing are not easily identified. It is, more generally, difficult to determine conclusively the extent to which Plato in the myth as a whole is reworking traditional ideas or imaginatively innovating. The treatment of Plato's eschatological myths at Frutiger 1930, 249–65, includes a table of parallels to be found in Empedocles, Pindar, and the Orphic tablets. Ebert 2014, 420–2, situates the *Phaedo* myth within the Italian-Sicilian tradition, the novel religiosity of which he finds expressed in the myths of Parmenides and Empedocles. Ebert also contends (425 ff.) that the account of the earth at 108c5–110a9 should be viewed as a bit of natural philosophy, the general truth of which Socrates indicates he has been persuaded, and that the mythical portion of Socrates' account only properly begins thereafter, with Socrates himself marking the transition with the words εἰ γὰρ δὴ καὶ μῦθον λέγειν καλόν (110a9–b1). Kingsley 1995, ch. 7, details numerous apparent parallels between the features of Plato's description of the subterranean phenomena and the geography of Sicily. His argument becomes more tenuous when he proceeds in chs. 8 and 9 to identify the Pythagoreanism of southern Italy and Sicily as the main source of the *Phaedo*'s eschatology. A useful corrective to the supposition that Plato is reproducing an existing Pythagorean doctrine of astral immortality is provided by Burkert 1972, 364–8.

[63] This notion that the philosophically virtuous and the more ordinarily virtuous souls will receive their distinct rewards has already been articulated at *Phd.* 80e2–81a10 and 82a11–c1.

permanent, and given its inherent relation to it, it comes to be ever with it (ἀεὶ μετ᾿ ἐκείνου τε γίγνεται)" (79d1–3). Socrates envisages that the temporary union of the soul with its objects that he had somewhat figuratively envisaged in the context of the affinity argument becomes an actual and lasting union once the philosophical soul has achieved its permanent release from bodily association.

Socrates concludes by impressing on Simmias that it is for the sake of this prospect that one must make every effort to partake of virtue and wisdom in this life – "for fair is the prize and great the hope" (114c6–9). If the soul is immortal, and if its fate depends on the condition it has achieved in its preceding life, then it is imperative to strive for the perfection and purification of the soul that consists in becoming as good and wise as possible. The surest path toward this end is the practice of philosophy. Socrates concludes his defense of the philo-sophical life with a critique of the counterfeit virtues of the hedonists and materialists, leading to the positive claim that only if one possesses wisdom can one be genuinely courageous, self-controlled, just, and, in sum, truly virtuous (68c5–69c3). Wisdom itself, he says, is a kind of purification (c2–3). The *Phaedo*'s ultimate aim is a defense of the philosophic life as the best and most beneficial of lives for a human being. Its defense should be compared to that of the *Republic*, which is developed through the bulk of the dialogue without attention to its external benefits or possible rewards in the afterlife. The *Phaedo*'s defense of the philosophic life does not exclude attention to those possible rewards – on the contrary, it justifies the philosophic life explicitly in terms of those rewards. Not only can the philosopher expect finally to attain the truth and understanding that has been the object of his most intense desire during his lifetime, but he can expect to enjoy the best possible fate in the afterlife. And yet his serene and happy confidence in the face of death is not due to his possessing any actual knowledge of what awaits, and not even due to his knowing based on proof that his soul is immortal, for he has no such proof. Socrates is instead confident in the face of death because he knows that he has taken the best possible care of his soul and has engaged throughout his life in the most worthwhile of activities.

References

Ackrill, J. L. 1973. "Anamnesis in the *Phaedo*: remarks on 73c–75c." In his *Essays on Plato and Aristotle*. Oxford: Oxford University Press, 1997: 13–32. Originally published in E. N. Lee et al., eds., *Exegesis and Argument*. Assen: Van Gorcum, 1973: 177–95.

Annas, Julia. 1982. "Plato's myths of judgement." *Phronesis*, 27: 119–43.

Ausland, Hayden. 1997. "On reading Plato mimetically." *American Journal of Philology*, 118: 371–416.

Bacon, Helen H. 1990. "The poetry of Phaedo." In M. Griffith and D. J. Mastronarde (eds.), *Cabinet of the Muses: Essays on Classical and Comparative Literature in Honor of Thomas G. Rosenmeyer*. Atlanta, GA: Scholars Press: 147–62.

Bailey, D. T. J. 2005. "Logic and music in Plato's *Phaedo*." *Phronesis*, 50: 95–115.

Baltussen, Han. 2015. "Strato of Lampsacus as a reader of Plato's *Phaedo*: his critique of the soul's immortality." In Sylvain Delcomminette, Pieter d'Hoine, and Marc-Antoine Gavray (eds.), *Ancient Readings of Plato's* Phaedo. Leiden and Boston, MA: Brill: 37–62.

Barnes, Jonathan. 1978. "Plato's cyclical argument." *Canadian Journal of Philosophy*, 8: 397–419. Repr. in J. Barnes, *Method and Metaphysics: Essays in Ancient Philosophy* I, ed. Maddalena Bonelli. Oxford: Clarendon Press, 2011: 303–22.

Bedu-Addo, J. T. 1979. "The role of the hypothetical method in the *Phaedo*." *Phronesis*, 24: 111–32.

Benson, Hugh H. 2015. *Clitophon's Challenge: Dialectic in Plato's* Meno, Phaedo, *and* Republic. Oxford and New York: Oxford University Press.

Betegh, Gabor. 2006. "Eschatology and cosmology: models and problems." In Maria Michela Sassi (ed.), *La costruzione del discorso filosofico nell-età dei presocratici*. Pisa: Edizioni della Normale: 27–50.

Betegh, Gabor. 2018. "Cosmic and human cognition in the *Timaeus*." In John Sisko (ed.), *Philosophy of Mind in Antiquity*. London: Routledge: 120–40.

Bett, Richard. 1986. "The argument for immortality in Plato's *Phaedrus*." *Phronesis*, 31: 1–26.

Blondell, Ruby. 2002. *The Play of Character in Plato's Dialogues*. Cambridge: Cambridge University Press.

Blyth, Dougal. 1997. "The ever-moving soul in Plato's *Phaedrus*." *American Journal of Philology*, 118: 185–217.

Bostock, David. 1986. *Plato's* Phaedo. Oxford: Clarendon Press.

Boys-Stones, George. 2004. "Phaedo of Elis and Plato on the soul." *Phronesis*, 49: 1–23.

Burkert, Walter. 1972. *Lore and Science in Ancient Pythagoreanism*, trans. E. L. Minar, Jr. Cambridge, MA: Harvard University Press.

Decleva Caizzi, F. 1970. "ἀεικίνητον ο αὐτοκίνητον?" *Acme*, 23: 91–7.

Denyer, Nicholas. 2007. "The *Phaedo*'s final argument." In Dominic Scott (ed.), *Maieusis: Essays on Ancient Philosophy in Honour of Myles Burnyeat*. Oxford: Oxford University Press: 87–96.

Dorter, Kenneth. 1982. *Plato's* Phaedo: *An Interpretation*. Toronto: University of Toronto Press.

Dorter, Kenneth. 2001. "'Deathless is indestructible: if not we need another argument': an implicit argument in the *Phaedo*." In Aleš Havlíček and Filip Karfík (eds.), *Plato's* Phaedo: *Proceedings of the Second Symposium Platonicum Pragense*. Prague: OIKOYMENH: 406–23.

Duke, E. A., W. F. Hicken, W. S. M. Nicoll, D. B. Robinson, and J. C. G. Strachan (eds.). 1995. *Platonis Opera I, Tetralogias I-II Continens*. Oxford: Clarendon Press.

Ebert, Theodor. 2001. "Sokrates über seinen Umgang mit Hypotheseis ('Phaidon' 100A): Ein Problem und ein Vorschlag zur Lösung." *Hermes*, 129(4): 467–73.

Ebert, Theodor. 2014. "'Wenn ich einen schönen Mythos vortragen darf . . .'. Zu Status, Herkunft und Funktion des Schlussmythos in Platons *Phaidon*." In Markus Janka and Christian Schäfer (eds.), *Platon als Mythologe: Interpretationen zu den Mythen in Platons Dialogen*, 2nd ed. Darmstadt: Wissenschaftliche Buchgesellschaft: 419–37.

Ebrey, David. 2013. "A new philosophical tool in the *Meno*: 86e–87c." *Ancient Philosophy*, 33: 75–96.

Edelstein, Ludwig. 1949. "The function of the myth in Plato's philosophy." *Journal of the History of Ideas*, 10: 463–81.

Edmonds, Radcliffe, G., III. 2004. *Myths of the Underworld Journey: Plato, Aristophanes, and the "Orphic" Gold Tablets*. Cambridge: Cambridge University Press.

Edmonds, Radcliffe, G., III. 2013. *Redefining Ancient Orphism: A Study in Greek Religion*. Cambridge: Cambridge University Press.

Fischer, Franck. 2002. "La méthode et les hypothèses en *Phédon* 99d–102a." *Revue Philosophique de Louvain*, 100: 650–80.

Franklin, Lee. 2005. "Recollection and philosophical reflection in Plato's *Phaedo*." *Phronesis*, 50: 289–314.

Frede, Dorothea. 1978. "The final proof of the immortality of the soul in Plato's *Phaedo* 102a–107a." *Phronesis*, 23: 24–41.

Frede, Dorothea. 2011. "Das Argument aus den essentiellen Eigenschaften (102a–107d)." In Jörn Müller (ed.), *Platon: Phaidon*. Berlin: Akademie Verlag: 143–57.

Frede, Michael. 1992. "Plato's arguments and the dialogue form." In James C. Klagge and Nicholas D. Smith (eds.), *Methods of Interpreting Plato and His Dialogues, Oxford Studies in Ancient Philosophy suppl. vol.* Oxford: Oxford University Press: 201–19.

Frutiger, Perceval. 1930. *Les mythes de Platon: Étude philosophique et littéraire*. Paris: Félix Alcan.

Gallop, David. 1975. *Plato: Phaedo. Translated with Notes*. Oxford: Clarendon Press.

Gallop, David. 1982. "Plato's 'cyclical argument' recycled." *Phronesis*, 27: 207–22.

Gentzler, Jyl. 1991. "συμφωνεῖν in Plato's *Phaedo*." *Phronesis*, 36: 265–76.

Gertz, Sebastian. 2015. "From 'immortal' to 'imperishable': Damascius on the final argument in Plato's *Phaedo*." In Sylvain Delcomminette, Pieter d'Hoine, and Marc-Antoine Gavray (eds.), *Ancient Readings of Plato's* Phaedo. Leiden and Boston, MA: Brill: 240–55.

Giannantoni, G. 1990. *Socratis et Socraticorum Reliquiae IV.* Naples: Bibliopolis.

Gottschalk, H. B. 1971. "Soul as harmonia." *Phronesis*, 16: 179–98.

Griswold, Charles L., Jr. 1988. *Platonic Writings/Platonic Readings*. New York and London: Routledge.

Hackforth, R. 1952. *Plato's* Phaedrus. Cambridge: Cambridge University Press.

Huffman, Carl A. 1993. *Philolaus of Croton: Pythagorean and Presocratic*. Cambridge: Cambridge University Press.

Inwood, Michael. 2009. "Plato's eschatological myths." In Catalin Partenie (ed.), *Plato's Myths*. Cambridge: Cambridge University Press: 28–50.

Isnardi Parente, M. 1977. "Le obiezioni di Stratone al *Fedone* e l'epistemologia peripatetica nel primo ellenismo." *Rivista di filologia e di istruzione classica*, 105: 285–306.

Iwata, Naoya. 2015. "Plato on geometrical hypothesis in the *Meno*." *Apeiron*, 48: 1–19.

Kanayama, Yahei. 2000. "The methodology of the second voyage and the proof of the soul's indestructibility in Plato's *Phaedo*." *Oxford Studies in Ancient Philosophy*, 18: 41–100.

Karasmanis, V. 2011. "Ἀπαγωγή: Hippocrates of Chios and Plato's hypothetical method in the *Meno*." In A. Longo (ed.), *Argument from Hypothesis in Ancient Philosophy, Elenchos* 59. Naples: Bibliopolis: 21–41.

Keyt, David. 1963. "The fallacies in *Phaedo* 102a–107b." *Phronesis*, 8: 167–72.

Kingsley, Peter. 1995. *Ancient Philosophy, Mystery, and Magic: Empedocles and the Pythagorean Tradition*. Oxford: Clarendon Press.

Lesser, A. H. 2003. "Unity of Plato's *Phaedo*." *Philosophical Inquiry*, 25: 73–85.

Lorenz, Hendrik. 2009. "Ancient theories of soul." *Stanford Encyclopedia of Philosophy*. http://plato.stanford.edu/archives/sum2009/entries/ancient-soul.

Mansfeld, Jaap. 2014. "Alcmaeon and Plato on soul." *Études platoniciennes* [online], 11: http://journals.openedition.org/etudesplatoniciennes/508.

McKirahan, Richard. 2016. "Philolaus on the soul." In Almut-Barbara Renger and Allessandro Stavru (eds.), *Pythagorean Knowledge from the Ancient to the Modern World: Askesis, Religion, Science*. Wiesbaden: Harrassowitz: 63–76.

Menn, Stephen. 2002. "Plato and the method of analysis." *Phronesis*, 47: 193–223.

Modrak, Deborah K. W. 2011. "Physicalism in Strato's psychology." In Marie-Laurence Desclos and William W. Fortenbaugh (eds.), *Strato of Lampsacus: Text, Translation, and Discussion*. New Brunswick, NJ, and London: Transaction Publishers: 383–97.

Morgan, Kathryn A. 2000. *Myth and Philosophy from the Presocratics to Plato*. Cambridge: Cambridge University Press.

Morgan, Michael L. 1984. "Sense-perception and recollection in the *Phaedo*." *Phronesis*, 29: 237–51.

Napolitano Valditara, Linda M. 1991. "τί ἐστιν – ποῖόν ἐστιν: un aspetto dell'argomentatività diallettica del *Menone*." *Elenchos*, 12: 197–220.

O'Brien, Denis. 1967. "The last argument of Plato's *Phaedo*. I." *The Classical Quarterly*, n.s. 17: 198–231.

O'Brien, Denis. 2007. "'Immortel' et 'impérissable' dans le *Phédon* de Platon." *The International Journal of the Platonic Tradition*, 1(2): 109–262.

Pakaluk, Michael. 2003. "Degrees of separation in the *Phaedo*." *Phronesis*, 48: 89–115.

Partenie, Catalin (ed.). 2009. *Plato's Myths*. Cambridge: Cambridge University Press.

Pender, Elizabeth. 2012. "The rivers of Tartarus: Plato's geography of dying and coming-back-to-life." In C. Collobert, P. Destrée, and F. J. Gonzalez (eds.), *Plato and Myth: Studies on the Use and Status of Platonic Myths*. Leiden and Boston, MA: Brill: 199–233.

Politis, V. 2010. "Explanation and essence in Plato's *Phaedo*." In D. Charles (ed.), *Definition in Greek Philosophy*. Oxford and New York: Oxford University Press: 62–114.

Robinson, T. M. 1971. "The argument for immortality in Plato's *Phaedrus*." In J. P. Anton and K. L. Kustas (eds.), *Essays in Ancient Greek Philosophy*. Albany, NY: State University of New York Press: 345–53.

Rosetti, Livio. 1980. "Ricerche sui 'Dialoghi Socratici' de Fedone e di Euclide." *Hermes*, 108: 183–200.

Rowe, C. J. 1993a. *Plato:* Phaedo. Cambridge: Cambridge University Press.

Rowe, C. J. 1993b. "Philosophy and literature: the arguments of Plato's *Phaedo*." In John J. Cleary (ed.), *Proceedings of the Boston Area Colloquium in Ancient Philosophy* 7. Lanham, MD and London: University Press of America: 159–181.

Sedley, David. 1991. "Teleology and myth in the *Phaedo*." *Proceedings of the Boston Area Colloquium in Ancient Philosophy*, 5: 359–83.

Sedley, David. 1995. "The dramatis personae of Plato's *Phaedo*." In Timothy Smiley (ed.), *Philosophical Dialogues: Plato, Hume, Wittgenstein – Proceedings of the British Academy*, 85: 3–26.

Sedley, David 1996. "Plato's *Phaedo* in the third century B.C." In *ΟΔΟΙ ΔΙΖΗΣΙΟΣ, le vie della ricerca: studi in onore di Francesco Adorno*. Florence: L. S. Olschki: 447–55.

Sedley, David. 2006. "Form-particular resemblance in Plato's *Phaedo*." *Proceedings of the Aristotelian Society*, 106: 311–27.

Sedley, David. 2009. "Three kinds of Platonic immortality." In Dorothea Frede and Burkhard Reis (eds.), *Body and Soul in Ancient Philosophy*. Berlin: De Gruyter: 145–62.

Sedley, David. 2012. "Plato's theory of change at *Phaedo* 70–71." In Richard Patterson, Vassilis Karasmanis, and Arnold Hermann (eds.), *Presocratics and Plato: Festschrift at Delphi in Honor of Charles Kahn*. Las Vegas/Zurich/Athens: Parmenides Publishing: 147–63.

Sharples, Robert W. 2011. "Strato of Lampsacus: the sources, texts and translations." In Marie-Laurence Desclos and William W. Fortenbaugh (eds.), *Strato of Lampsacus: Text, Translation, and Discussion*. New Brunswick, NJ and London: Transaction Publishers: 5–229.

Smyth, Herbert W. 1920. *Greek Grammar*. Cambridge, MA: Harvard University Press.

Strachan, J. C. G. 1970. "Who did forbid suicide at *Phaedo* 62b?" *The Classical Quarterly*, 20: 216–20.

Svavarsson, Svavar Hrafn. 2009. "Plato on Forms and conflicting appearances: the argument of *Phaedo* 74a9–c6." *Classical Quarterly*, 59: 60–74.

Warren, James. 2001. "Socratic suicide." *The Journal of Hellenic Studies*, 121: 91–106.

Warren, James. 2006. "Psychic disharmony: Philoponus and Epicurus on Plato's *Phaedo*." *Oxford Studies in Ancient Philosophy*, 30: 235–59.

Weller, C. 1995. "Fallacies in the *Phaedo* again." *Archiv für Geschichte der Philosophie*, 77: 121–34.

Westerink. L. G. 1977. *The Greek Commentaries on Plato's* Phaedo, vol. 2: *Damascius*. Amsterdam: North-Holland.

White, F. C. 2006. "Socrates, philosophers and death: two contrasting arguments in Plato's *Phaedo*." *The Classical Quarterly*, 56: 445–58.

Acknowledgments

Earlier versions of this work have benefited from discussion by audiences at the University of Pittsburgh, Indiana University, the University of South Carolina, the 2003 Pacific Division Meeting of the APA, and Princeton University. I am particularly grateful to Hugh Benson, Tad Brennan, Charles Brittain, Michael Frede, David Gallop, Adam Leite, Tiberiu Popa, David Sedley, Evanthia Speliotis, and Steven Strange for their comments on its various versions and to Geoffrey Lloyd and David Sedley for probing comments on its original precursor. I am likewise grateful to series editor James Warren and the Press' anonymous reviewer for their suggestions.

Cambridge Elements ☰

Ancient Philosophy

James Warren
University of Cambridge

James Warren is Professor of Ancient Philosophy at the University of Cambridge. He is the author of *Epicurus and Democritean Ethics* (Cambridge, 2002), *Facing Death: Epicurus and His Critics* (2004), *Presocratics* (2007), and *The Pleasures of Reason in Plato, Aristotle and the Hellenistic Hedonists* (Cambridge, 2014). He is also the editor of *The Cambridge Companion to Epicurus* (Cambridge, 2009), and joint editor of *Authors and Authorities in Ancient Philosophy* (Cambridge, 2018).

About the Series

The Elements in Ancient Philosophy series deals with a wide variety of topics and texts in ancient Greek and Roman philosophy, written by leading scholars in the field. Taking a theme, question, or type of argument, some Elements explore it across antiquity and beyond. Others look in detail at an ancient author, a specific work, or a part of a longer work, considering its structure, content, and significance, or explore more directly ancient perspectives on modern philosophical questions.

Cambridge Elements ☰

Ancient Philosophy

Printed in the United States
By Bookmasters